From Gates to Apps

From Gates to Apps

*What Every High School Student
Needs to Know About Computer Science*

Edward G. Amoroso
Matthew E. Amoroso

SILICON PRESS
Summit, NJ 07901
www.silicon-press.com

Silicon Press
Summit, NJ 07901
USA

First Edition
Printing 5 4 3 2 1   Year 17 16 5 14 13

ISBN10: 0-929306-53-8
ISBN13: 978-0-929306-53-7

Library of Congress Cataloging-in-Publication Data
Amoroso, Edward G.
  From gates to apps : what every high school student needs to know about computer science / Edward Amoroso, Matthew Amoroso.
        pages cm
  Includes bibliographical references and index.
  ISBN 978-0-929306-53-7 (alkaline paper)
 1. Computer science--Textbooks.   I. Amoroso, Matthew. II. Title.
  QA76.A584 2013
  004--dc23   2013021630

Contents

Preface

We must be very careful when we give advice to younger people: sometimes they follow it!

Edsger Dijkstra

Most computer science textbooks for young people focus on the use of programming languages such as Java or Python. The driving force behind this emphasis on coding, presumably, is that students have neither the interest nor the attention span to learn about important low-level computing concepts such as logic gates or memory design.

While it is true that most grade school and high school students have become accustomed to the fast pace and visual barrage of on-line gaming, mobile applications, and video, the potential remains that fundamental concepts can still provide some excitement. This is especially true for any youngster or hobbyist interested in what *really* occurs under the hood in a computer system.

Consider this: In the United States alone, there are a nearly quarter of a billion people walking around with mobile devices, a rapidly growing portion of which are smart phones. The vast majority of these mobile users – in fact, virtually all of them – have no idea what makes these devices run. Most could barely explain what a central processing unit *is*, much less how one works.

In an era where dependence on software, computers, and networks continues to grow, every nation needs to nurture its youth with the most valuable and relevant technology education. This book was written with that goal in mind. It is intended as a bottoms-up introduction to a topic that every youngster should understand, especially those considering a future career in technology.

It seems ironic that we demand that high school students study biology and chemistry, both valid disciplines, but we are not shocked when young people graduate from high school – and even college – with no understanding of computing. In the United States, in particular, this omission of computing technology from a young person's basic education will not serve us well in the coming decades.

Written from the unique combined perspective of the professional computer scientist, professor, and author (Edward) and the current high school student, addicted gamer, and programmer (Matthew), the book introduces fundamental concepts in a way that should be accessible to young minds. It uses short, simple explanations with diagrams to introduce concepts in a straightforward way.

Starting with the basics of binary numbers and logic gates, the book shows how computing components such as memory and central processing units are designed, along with a simple model of computers. From there, the book outlines programming constructs along with rudimentary algorithms. The final part introduces larger concepts such as operating systems, networks, and the Internet.

Hopefully, students using this book will come away with a high-level, initial view of the types of technical underpinnings that will be necessary to be successful in the next century. It should help to lead at least some of them to a lifetime of interest in a critically important topic to all nations: *computer science*.

E.A., M.A
Byram Township, NJ
July, 2013

1: Binary Numbers

There are only 10 kinds of people in the world, those who understand binary, and those who don't.

Anonymous

To properly understand *computer science*, you need to first understand the concept of a *number system,* which is the standard notation for representing *numbers*. As you'll learn, different number systems exist, including the familiar *decimal system* used by humans, as well as the less familiar *binary system* used by computers.

The decimal system, also known as *base-ten*, is the one humans use every day. Mathematicians speculate that we use decimal because it includes ten symbols, which corresponds to the ten fingers on our hands. The symbols used in decimal look like this:

0　1　2　3　4　5　6　7　8　9

While humans use these ten symbols to count and perform calculations, they generally begin counting from 1 rather than 0, unlike computer scientists who prefer to count from 0 (for reasons that will become clearer when we study *computer memory*). Thus, if a typical human being had one item in each hand, then the two items would be counted as follows:

1　2

Counting using decimal is familiar, because it is how we're taught as small children. We learn, for example, that when we add 1 to 9, we run out of new symbols, so we use the 1 and 0 symbols to create 10. The same goes for adding 1 to 99 to get 100, or for adding 1 to 99,999 to get 100,000.

Computers, as should be obvious, do not have ten fingers. One might suggest instead that computers have something that corresponds more to having *two* fingers. That is, the underlying electronics used in computer systems are switches that can be in two positions – *on* and *off*. So the motivation exists to find some different number system that is more compatible with how computers operate.

Let's look at a number system different than decimal. If we imagine that the symbol 9 does not exist, then the corresponding *base-nine* number system would include these symbols:

0   1   2   3   4   5   6   7   8

Using this number system, here's how you would count decimal ten items:

1   2   3   4   5   6   7   8   10   11

Notice that in base-nine without a 9 symbol, we must reuse the 1 and 0 symbols earlier. Suppose now that the 9 and 8 symbols were both non-existent. Here is how we would count decimal ten items in *base-eight*:

1   2   3   4   5   6   7   10   11   12

Following the same logic, we can create *base-seven*, *base-six*, *base-five*, *base-four*, *base-three*, and *base-two* number systems. This is done by successively removing the highest symbol used in counting. When we get down to the *base-two* or *binary* number system, we find that exactly two symbols remain for counting, namely 0 and 1.

Example: If we have decimal four items in each of our hands, how many items do we have in the base-three number system?

Answer: Having decimal four items in each hand corresponds to a total of decimal eight items. The base-three representation of decimal eight is as follows:

1   2   10   11   12   20   21   22

Thus, if we have decimal four items in each hand, then we would say that we have a total of 22 items in the base-three number system.

Computers operate using the *base-two* number system where only 0's and 1's are used. As suggested above, the switches in the design of a computer can be *on* or *off.* If you represent an *on* switch as a 1, and an *off* switch as a 0, then you can count or compute in binary with switches.

Thus, if we want to use base-two to count decimal ten items, it would look as follows:

1   10   11   100   101   110   111   1000   1001   1010

A useful table of translations for the decimal numbers from 0 to 10 to their binary equivalents is below:

Decimal	0	Binary	0
Decimal	1	Binary	1
Decimal	2	Binary	10
Decimal	3	Binary	11
Decimal	4	Binary	100
Decimal	5	Binary	101
Decimal	6	Binary	110
Decimal	7	Binary	111
Decimal	8	Binary	1000
Decimal	9	Binary	1001
Decimal	10	Binary	1010

Procedures are often created for translating arbitrary numbers from one number system to another. Usually, these procedures will translate binary numbers to decimal, for when humans need to read them, and from decimal numbers to binary, when computers need to use them. The translations also often include other number systems such as *hexadecimal* or *base-sixteen* (explained later).

One technique for converting binary to decimal involves *powers of two*. The way the *powers of two* technique works is that we look for places where there is a 1 in the binary number, and we then calculate the value of the power of two in that place. Once we have calculated all the powers of two for every place in the binary where there is a 1, we then add up all the respective values to obtain the final answer.

The diagram below shows how this step-by-step procedure for converting binary to decimal would work for converting the binary number 0001 0101 to its decimal equivalent:

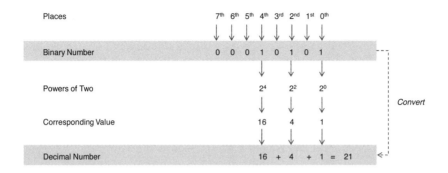

To convert decimal to binary, we start by identifying the largest power of two that fits into the decimal. For example, if the decimal number is 25, then the largest *power of two* that fits into 25 is 2^4 which is 16. Repeating the procedure with the remainder, we see that 2^3 is now the largest power of two that fits. Finishing the procedure with the final remainder, we see that 2^0 fits into 1. We now compose the binary equivalent of 25 by placing a 1 in the 4th, 3rd, and 0th place of the binary – hence, decimal 25 is binary 00011001.

Now, let's perform some simple binary arithmetic by adding the binary representations of decimal 4 and decimal 3. We know that decimal 4 plus decimal 3 is decimal 7. Thus, using binary numbers, we are adding binary 100 to binary 011, which should result in the binary equivalent of decimal 7. This results in the following:

```
      100           -- Binary 100 is decimal 4.
   +  011           -- Binary 11 is decimal 3.
      ------
      111           -- The answer is binary 111 or decimal 7.
```

Just like in decimal arithmetic, adding binary numbers sometimes requires carrying digits over. So if we add binary 1 and binary 1 (show below with leading 0's) we get the following:

```
      0001          -- Binary 0001 is the same as binary 1
   +  0001          -- We add and have to carry the 1.
      ------
      0010          -- Binary 1 plus 1 equals 10, or decimal 2.
```

Example: Add decimal 3 to decimal 6 using the binary system.

Answer: We know that decimal 3 in binary is 11, and that decimal 6 in binary is 110. We can add the two as follows:

```
    0011          -- Use leading zeros to allow for carries.
  + 0110          -- Add and carry over to the next column.
  ---------
    1001          -- Binary 1001 is decimal 9.
```

If you practice using and working with binary numbers, then you'll find that you can start memorizing and using some familiar ones. You might try, for example, asking your parents for 1000 dollars. If they deny the request, which they will, then you can lower the amount by changing the number system. That is, if you ask for 1000 dollars in binary, then you're really just asking for decimal eight dollars, which you are more likely to get.

2: Hexadecimal Numbers

Question: If only DEAD people know hexadecimal, then how many is that? Answer: 57005.

Anonymous

L et's continue our study of number systems by counting to decimal 16 from 1:

1   2   3   4   5   6   7   8   9   10   11   12   13   14   15   16

Where we *removed* symbols for number systems such as binary, we can also add symbols to create other number systems. Thus, in addition to the decimal symbols from 0 to 9, we might add new symbols for higher numbers. To make things simple, we can use capital letters as these new symbols.

To start, suppose that the symbol A represents what we normally think of as decimal ten. Everything else would be the same, except that this new symbol would be used after 9. Here's how we would count to decimal sixteen if we included this new symbol:

1   2   3   4   5   6   7   8   9   A   10   11   12   13   14   15

You can see that if we count to decimal twenty-two using this new system, the A symbol comes into play in an interesting way, creating a new pattern:

Decimal System:
1 2 3 4 5 6 7 8 9 10 11 12 13 14 15 16 17 18 19 20 21 22

New System:
1 2 3 4 5 6 7 8 9 A 10 11 12 13 14 15 16 17 18 19 1A 20

If we now add the symbol B for what would normally be decimal eleven, we would count to decimal sixteen in this new number system as follows:

1 2 3 4 5 6 7 8 9 A B 10 11 12 13 14

Example: Using the number system that includes the symbols A and B as shown above, count how many items you'd have if you had decimal six in one hand and decimal five in another.

Answer: If you have six items in one hand and five in another, then you would say that you had eleven or 11 using the decimal system. However, with the new symbols A and B, we would count the items as shown below:

1 2 3 4 5 6 7 8 9 A B

Thus, in our new number system with the symbols A and B, we would say that we have exactly B items.

Let's now make a new table starting with the decimal numbers and continuing until we've introduced a new symbol for all the numbers up to decimal fifteen. We'll just keep our naming system going with capital letters from A to F, and we will also leave off the initial 0 symbol since this is generally not going to be used in counting items:

1	2	3	4	5	6	7	8	9	10	11	12	13	14	15	16
1	2	3	4	5	6	7	8	9	A	10	11	12	13	14	15
1	2	3	4	5	6	7	8	9	A	B	10	11	12	13	14
1	2	3	4	5	6	7	8	9	A	B	C	10	11	12	13
1	2	3	4	5	6	7	8	9	A	B	C	D	10	11	12
1	2	3	4	5	6	7	8	9	A	B	C	D	E	10	11
1	2	3	4	5	6	7	8	9	A	B	C	D	E	F	10

Again, this table is the reverse of what we did in our discussion on binary numbers. The most important row in this table is the last one. It is written in the *base-sixteen* or *hexadecimal* number system. Here's how we would count items in hexadecimal:

1 2 3 4 5 6 7 8 9 A B C D E F 10

If we had a total of decimal sixteen items, then we would say that we had 10 items using base-sixteen or hexadecimal. If you asked your parents for ten bucks in hexadecimal and they agreed, then you would get the decimal equivalent of sixteen dollars.

Like binary, hexadecimal is one of the most important number systems in computer science. It is a system that computer science students learn to become as comfortable with as decimal. Here's why:

Anyone who owns an iPod, computer, smart phone, or gaming system knows that information is stored in *memory*. Memory in a computer is represented as a sequence of 0's and 1's arranged in patterns called *words* of eight binary numbers. This means that a chunk of words in the memory of a computer might look like this:

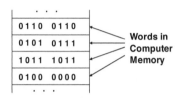

The reason words are eight bits has to do with how binary information can be extended to represent information. This is done in a manner related to *powers of two*. That is, a single bit can represent two pieces of information 0 or 1. Two bits can represent four pieces of information – namely, 00, 01, 10, or 11. Three bits can represent eight pieces of information, and so on.

These representations are derived from the powers of 2. Namely, one bit can represent 2^1 pieces of information; two bits can represent 2^2 pieces of information; three bits can represent 2^3 pieces of information; and so on. Computer system designers thus create memory using numbers that are powers of 2. Hexadecimal makes it more convenient for human beings to read binary memory in a computer. Note that hexadecimal, or *base sixteen*, also corresponds to a power of 2, namely, 2^4. Below is a conversion table for hexadecimal numbers from 0 to F:

Binary 0000   Hexadecimal 0
Binary 0001   Hexadecimal 1
Binary 0010   Hexadecimal 2
Binary 0011   Hexadecimal 3
Binary 0100   Hexadecimal 4
Binary 0101   Hexadecimal 5
Binary 0110   Hexadecimal 6

Binary 0111   Hexadecimal   7
Binary 1000   Hexadecimal   8
Binary 1001   Hexadecimal   9
Binary 1010   Hexadecimal   A
Binary 1011   Hexadecimal   B
Binary 1100   Hexadecimal   C
Binary 1101   Hexadecimal   D
Binary 1110   Hexadecimal   E
Binary 1111   Hexadecimal   F

One key issue in the use of hexadecimal numbers in computers is that binary numbers are often referenced in hexadecimal as a short-hand. When computer scientists want to reference the value of memory, they don't calculate the value of every memory element, but rather just point to adjacent four-bit words which can be referenced using hexadecimal. This is illustrated in the example below.

Example: Using hexadecimal numbers, list the respective contents of the two adjacent eight-bit words of memory shown below:

0000 0001
1111 1110

Answer: The answer is determined by reading each binary word and converting to hexadecimal. Thus, binary 0000 is hexadecimal 0; binary 0001 is hexadecimal 1; binary 1111 is hexadecimal F; and binary 1110 is hexadecimal E. Most computer scientists would thus refer to the memory contents using hexadecimal as 01FE.

Words in memory can also be arranged into sequences of special codes called *instructions*. So, when you download software for your computer, you're really downloading an unbelievably long sequence of 0's and 1's that your system will interpret as instructions.

Base-two and base-sixteen numbers are the languages of computing, and if you get comfortable with these systems, you'll be well on your way to being able to converse with a computer scientist.

3: Logic Gates: NOT Gate

Did you hear the one about the logic gate that walks into a bar? NOT.

Anonymous

Now that we have some idea of how number systems work, we will begin investigating how computers are designed and how they operate. Most of the next few chapters will use binary numbers, and sometimes decimal and hexadecimal, to introduce the basic computing concepts.

Mathematicians use *operations* to perform computations. Common arithmetic operations include adding, subtracting, multiplying, and dividing. For example, when we perform the decimal computation: $2 + 2 = 4$, we've actually used the addition operation on decimal 2 and 2 to produce the result 4. Similarly, when we perform the subtraction computation: $4 - 3 = 1$, we've used the subtraction operation on decimal 4 and 3 to produce the result 1.

Computer scientists also use operations, but in a slightly different way. Adding, for example, is viewed as an operation that takes two *inputs* and produces an *output*. Thus, adding 6 and 8 would involve an addition operation on inputs 6 and 8 producing output 14. This would be depicted as follows:

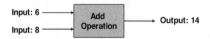

Similar operations can be defined for any function that takes one or more inputs and produces one or more outputs. It is worth reminding ourselves that *functions* always produce the same output for common input. This makes functions repeatable, which is an important consideration in computer system design and operation. As you will see, functional components are the basis for most computer system design.

Example: What is the result of performing the multiplication operation on binary inputs 0000 and 1010?

Answer: The multiplication operation always produces output zero when any of the inputs are zero. Thus, the multiplication operation on 0000 and 1010 produces 0000. This could be depicted in the diagram above by replacing inputs 6 and 8 with 0000 and 1010 and replacing the output 14 with output 0000. (Note that throughout this book that we will represent zero by writing 0, 00, 0000, or some other string of 0's depending on the context, even though they all obviously have the same value.)

Computers are designed from electronic components that perform operations on binary inputs to produce binary outputs. One of the simplest implementations of a numeric operation in a computer is the *logic gate* or just *gate*. A gate is an electronic device that can take any number of binary inputs, although one or two are most common, and produces a binary output. In this book, we will stick mostly to logic gates taking one or two inputs.

Gates are represented pictorially in diagrams using special symbols that correspond to each type of gate. The easiest gate is the **NOT** gate, which is shown symbolically as a triangle with a small circle in front (see below). This gate reverses an input 1 to an output 0, and an input 0 to an output 1. It's a simple process known as an *invert* operation. The picture below depicts the *invert* operation of a NOT gate.

Input 1 ──▷○── Output 0   Input 0 ──▷○── Output 1

When we examine the input and output behavior of a gate, we are presuming instantaneous production of an output. There is no delay from the time an input is presented to a gate to the time an output is presented.

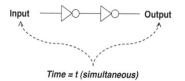

Input ──▷○──▷○── Output

Time = t (simultaneous)

We know that time is not an issue because our underlying implementation is electronic, and for all intents and purposes, the flow of electricity to a human being is essentially instantaneous. Certainly in real settings, especially if long networks across a large geography are introduced, then delays can occur. But for now, we will assume that in the small scale design of electronic components in a computer, that everything is instantaneous.

To describe the operation of a NOT gate, we had to draw the diagram above twice, once for each input. This can be inconvenient for more complex gates, so computer scientists often use *truth tables* to describe gate functions. A truth table shows, in tabular form, all possible inputs and their corresponding outputs. Below is the truth table for the NOT gate:

NOT Gate:

Input	Output
0	1
1	0

Now let's connect some NOT gates to demonstrate connectivity of different gates. Suppose, for example, that we connect two NOT gates together in series, with the output of the first NOT gate feeding into the input of the other. Here is a drawing of what this looks like:

In this arrangement, the input to the first NOT gate is first inverted. It then instantaneously becomes input to the second NOT gate which inverts it again. The result is that it is inverted twice. So, the dual-connected NOT gates have the result of performing a *repeat* operation, which does not change the value of the input. In computer science, we refer to this sort of device as a *repeater*. The truth table is shown below:

Repeater:

Input	Output
0	0
1	1

Any *even* number of NOT gates arranged in series will always result in a repeater. Similarly, any *odd* number of NOT gates in series will always produce the NOT truth table.

Example: What is the truth table that corresponds to three NOT gates in series?

Answer: Three NOT gates would have the following effect on input:

1) The first NOT gate would invert the input.
2) The second NOT gate would cancel out the first by inverting again.
3) The third NOT gate would then invert the output of the second gate.

So, the truth table would be exactly the same as for a single NOT gate (as shown previously in this discussion).

A branch of mathematics known as *Boolean algebra* helps in the modeling and analysis of gate logic. In Boolean algebra, all variables are either 0 or 1 unlike normal algebra. The operations in Boolean algebra include NOT, as well as the related AND and OR operations, which we will examine in the next chapter. Just as with normal algebra, basic laws such as the commutative, associative, and distributive laws can be established and derived.

As you progress in your study of computer science, you will learn how useful Boolean algebra can be in the design and analysis of more complex logic gate structures. It is the mathematical language used to design the components used to design, analyze, and build computer systems.

4: AND and OR Gates

Simplicity is prerequisite for reliability.

Edsger Dijkstra

I n this chapter, we introduce two new logic gates that each take two binary inputs and produce one binary output. The first of our new gates is a device known as an *AND gate*. The schematic and truth table are shown below:

AND Gate: Schematic

A ─────╮
        ╠──── C
B ─────╯

AND Gate: Truth Table

A	B	C
0	0	0
0	1	0
1	0	0
1	1	1

The operation of an AND gate is implied by its name. The only way the output can be a 1 is if the first input *and* the second input are 1. If either input is a 0, then the output is a zero. Below are descriptions of the four input combinations and the resultant output:

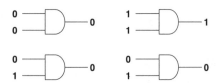

You can see that if the two inputs are *not* both 1, then the output is always zero. This behavior allows computer scientists to connect multiple AND gates into more interesting combinations of inputs and outputs. We did this with NOT gates in the previous chapter, but since AND gates take

14

two inputs to produce a single output, connecting multiple AND gates is slightly more involved.

Example: Describe the behavior of three AND gates combined to create a gate structure where the outputs of two AND gates become the inputs to the third gate.

Answer: Drawing the gate structure with the three AND gates results in four inputs producing a single output as follows:

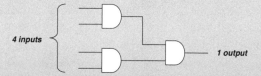

The behavior of this gate structure can be described by analyzing all possibilities of the four inputs from 0, 0, 0, 0 to 1, 1, 1, 1. Each input possibility produces interim outputs for the two initial AND gates, which in turn become the two inputs to the third AND gate. So, for example, if the inputs are all 0, as shown below, then the interim outputs are 0, which in turn produce an output in the third gate of 0.

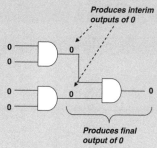

Using this type of logical analysis, it should be obvious that any input combination that includes a 0 *anywhere* will result in the final output being 0. The only input combination that will result in an output of 1 involves all four inputs being 1.

Now, let's introduce the second of our new logic gates, a useful device that is known as an *OR gate*. Its schematic and truth table are shown below:

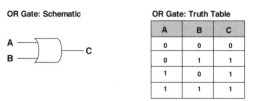

OR Gate: Schematic

OR Gate: Truth Table

A	B	C
0	0	0
0	1	1
1	0	1
1	1	1

The operation of an OR gate is also implied by its name. The output of this gate will be a 1 if the first *or* second input is 1. The only way the output of an OR gate can be 0 is if both inputs are 1. Another way of saying this is that the output of the OR gate is 1 as long as one of the inputs is 1. As such, it is a useful gate for detecting a 1 value as one of the inputs. A gate diagram of all possibilities is shown below:

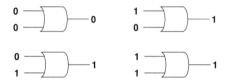

If three OR gates are combined (similar to the three AND gate combination in the example above), the result is a gate structure that will produce output 1 only if any of the inputs is 1. This combined logic gate arrangement looks as follows:

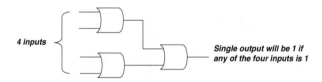

4 inputs

Single output will be 1 if any of the four inputs is 1

Computer scientists often use AND and OR gates as *models* to design simple computing applications. While the actual AND and OR gate functions in a typical computer would be deeply embedded into the function of something know as the *central processing unit* (CPU) of the computer, it is certainly possible to purchase tiny electronic AND and OR gate functions packaged into electronic components called *chips*. A computer chip looks like this:

These pins are the
inputs, outputs, and other
useful functions of the chip

These computer chips can be used to create useful electronic configurations. For example, by placing a simple light switch in front of each input to a gate and then connecting the output to a small light, we can visually depict the operation of the gate. The diagram below shows such an arrangement for an OR gate.

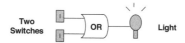

Two
Switches   OR   Light

The logic in the above arrangement follows the way an OR gate works. The two inputs are interpreted as switches. So, if you turn on either of the two switches, the OR gate would then turn the light on. The only way the light can possibly be off would be for both switches to also be off. It's not hard to imagine how this function might be used in many types of real-life applications.

In computer design, logic gates are connected to *electronic circuits* so that inputs and outputs can be represented by electronic *voltages*. You might have learned a bit about voltages in science class in school, but for now you can think about voltages as measures of energy potential when a power source like a battery is present in the circuit.

In a computer, binary 1 will be represented by the presence of positive 5 volts in a circuit, and a binary 0 will be represented by the presence of 0 volts in the circuit. By varying the voltages into and out of gates, computers can be designed to perform useful operations. The diagram below shows a typical representation of varying voltage levels.

Voltage
Levels

+5 volts – – ➤

0 volts – – ➤

Suppose, for example, that the switches in the diagram above instantaneously generate either 5 volts (when turned on) or 0 volts (when turned off), and also that the light goes on in the presence of 5 volts, and off when no voltage is present. We can now redraw the diagram with the switches connected to the inputs of the OR gate and the light connected to the output as follows:

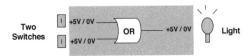

This diagram is an accurate depiction of what goes on inside the components that make up a computer. Devices and computer components accept and generate 5 volt or 0 volt inputs and outputs; and in this way, they can utilize and generate binary inputs and outputs. As we've suggested several times already, keep in mind that all of this occurs essentially instantaneously with no delay between input and output. When we get to somewhat trickier arrangements of logic gates combined together, the idea of simultaneity will be an important consideration in trying to understand the function of some component.

5: Combining Gates

Life is really simple, but we insist on making it complicated.

Confucius

We showed above how to combine gates together into more complex structures. We did this by making the outputs of one or more gates the respective inputs to another gate. The analysis of these types of combinations is central to computer design and is also one of the fundamental concepts of computer science. The connections between different gates, and in fact between any components of a computer system, are referred to as *interfaces*.

Let's continue our investigation of combining gates into more complex structures by first introducing a new type of logic gate called NAND that reverses the binary output of an AND gate. The schematic and truth table for the NAND gate look like this:

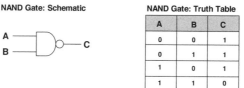

NAND Gate: Schematic	NAND Gate: Truth Table

A	B	C
0	0	1
0	1	1
1	0	1
1	1	0

The NAND gate is important because its output is 0 whenever its inputs are 1, and its output is 1 for all other input combinations. You could think of the NAND gate as a device that detects when all inputs are 1 or turned on by producing a 0 output. It is also useful for detecting the presence of some 0 input – which is the reverse of the AND gate. Analyzing all the possible inputs to the NAND gate diagrammatically produces the following four cases:

As you'd expect, the output of an OR gate can also be reversed in a gate called NOR. This gate produces a 0 output whenever either of the inputs is 1. It also produces a 1 output whenever both inputs are 0. The schematic for a NOR is shown below in the context of the four different input combinations:

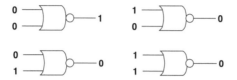

So now, let's look at what happens when we combine logic gates into different types of logical arrangements. Below is a simple gate structure that uses one NOT gate and one AND gate:

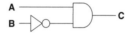

To determine the truth table, we need to do a bit of simple analysis on the inputs A and B. Whenever A is 0, the output C will be 0, because an AND gate always has output 0 when either input is 0. So, for the output C to be 1, A must be 1, and B must be 0, because its value is reversed by the NOT gate. Using this logic on the inputs, here is the truth table for this simple two-gate structure:

Truth Table:

A	B	C
0	0	0
0	1	0
1	0	1
1	1	0

Example: Describe the behavior of a gate structure where two inputs A and B are directly connected to NOT gates, which then become the respective inputs to an AND gate.

Answer: Drawing the gate structure with the two NOT gates and the single AND gate results in the following:

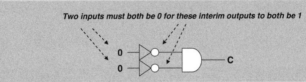

The behavior of this gate structure can be described by analyzing the possibilities of inputs. If the two inputs A and B are both 0, then the interim outputs from the two NOT gates will both be 1. Any other combination of inputs will result in at least one output being 0. The interim output result from the two NOT gates thus looks like this:

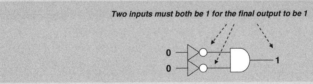

We can further visualize the relationship between the outputs of the two NOT gates and the inputs to the AND gate as follows:

Two inputs must both be 1 for the final output to be 1

Using this logic, it should be obvious that any input combination that includes a 1 will result in the final output being 0. The only input combination that will result in an output of 1 involves both original inputs being 0.

It might not be immediately evident why different logical combination of gates would be useful, but in computer circuit design, one might need different functions for a given component. Let's now look at a slightly more complex combination of gates. This time, we'll include two AND gates and one NOT gate in the structure. Furthermore, in this arrangement, the A input will be split into two equal inputs to the first AND gate:

If the value of A is 1, then both inputs to the AND gate are 1. Similarly, if the value of A is 0, then both inputs to the AND gate are 0. When B is 0, the output to the second AND gate must always be 0; but since this is reversed by the NOT gate, whenever B is 0, C is always 1. Also, when B is 1 and A is 0, the output from the second AND gate will be 0, but it is reversed, so the output is 1. Hence, for C to be 0, both A and B must be 1. Here is the resultant truth table:

Truth Table:

A	B	C
0	0	1
0	1	1
1	0	1
1	1	0

This truth table describes exactly the function of the NAND gate we introduced at the start of this discussion. As such, the gate arrangement shown above could be replaced with a NAND gate. In computer system design, this replacement of something complicated with something less complex is known as *simplification*. If you were designing a component that relied on use of the above combination, you could simplify it as follows:

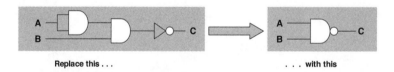

Replace this . . .   . . . with this

Example: Replace the following serial connection of five NOT gates with a simpler gate structure:

Answer: Since each pair of NOT gates corresponds to a simple repeater (essentially cancelling each other out), and since the serial connection include five NOT gates (which is odd), the entire connection can be replaced with a single NOT gate. In any design that includes a serial pattern of NOT gates such as shown above, odd numbers of NOT gates should be replaced more simply with a single NOT gate, and even numbers of NOT gates should be simply removed.

The process of design simplification is regarded by computer scientists as an important practice. Perhaps the greatest computer scientist, *Edsger Dijkstra*, once referred to the primary goal of computer science as *reducing complexity*. Without a great deal of attention focused on making things as simple as possible, the likelihood of design errors creeping into computer systems becomes very high.

6: SR-Latch

Other kids went and beat each other up, or played
baseball, and I built electronics.

Robert Moog

Perhaps the most commonly recognized aspect of any computer is its *memory*. This is the portion of a computer that makes it possible to store applications, download music, and save pictures. If you've ever purchased a computer, smart phone, or other electronic device, then you already know that you pay more money for more memory. This should help you understand how important it is to create efficient and cost-effective means for creating memory devices.

In the memory of a computer, information is stored as sequences of binary data, where each 0 or 1 in the binary sequence is referred to as a *bit*. As you would expect, computer scientists have designed *memory cells* based on logic gates that are used to store bits of information. By lining up memory devices, designers can create sequences of memory cells that are embedded into computers as shown below:

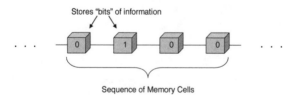

Sequence of Memory Cells

Memory cells are useful in a computer because they can be used for simple operations that involve a bit being provided as *input* to the cell, or a bit being produced as *output* from the cell. This implies that the memory exists in the context of other logical devices that can perform such operations. To make things simple, and consistent with our discussion previously, you can think of input as being voltage levels on wires that are connected to the memory cell. You can also imagine other inputs and outputs being connected to a memory cell to help control how it operates.

One of the most basic logical implementations of a memory cell in a computer is called a *set-reset latch* or *SR-Latch*. An SR-Latch has two inputs and two outputs as follows:

The Set and Reset connections to the SR-Latch are its inputs, and the Q and Q' connections from the SR-Latch are its outputs. The operation of an SR-Latch is simple: The Q output is the value of the bit stored in memory and the Q' output is always the *complement* or opposite of the Q value. This means that when the value of Q is 1, we can interpret the SR-Latch as storing a 1; similarly, if the value of Q is 0, then we interpret this as a stored 0 in the SR-Latch. Below is the interpretation for Q set to 1:

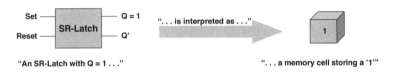

Similarly, we can set Q to 0, which has the interpretation of storing a 0 in the memory cell, as shown below:

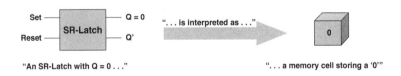

The Set and Reset connections to the SR-Latch are used as inputs that can cause the SR-Latch value to be either 1 or 0, depending on what is needed. The Set input places the value of 1 into the SR-Latch, and the Reset input resets the value to 0. The one stipulation is that the device does not allow both setting and resetting at the same time. There are three different configurations of inputs that can be used in an SR-Latch:

- Inputs: *Set = 1* and *Reset = 0*: Outputs: *Q becomes 1* and *Q' becomes 0*

- Inputs: *Set = 0* and *Reset = 1*: Outputs: *Q becomes 0 and Q'*
  becomes 1
- Inputs: *Set = 0* and *Reset = 0*: Outputs: *Q and Q' are not changed.*
- Inputs*: Set = 1* and *Reset = 1*: This input configuration not used by
  SR-Latch

As you can see, the Set = 1 and Reset = 0 inputs force the output
value Q to be set to 1. Similarly, the Reset = 1 and Set = 0 inputs force the
output value for Q to be set to 0. This operation can be viewed as storing
binary information into memory. Also, when 0 is applied to both inputs, the
values of Q and Q' are not changed. The SR-Latch does not use the input
configuration where both Set and Reset are 1. The circuit designer must be
careful to make sure that these inputs are not applied to the SR-Latch.

Example: What are the binary and decimal representations of the following
sequence of four SR-Latch Q values (listed from 1 to 4):

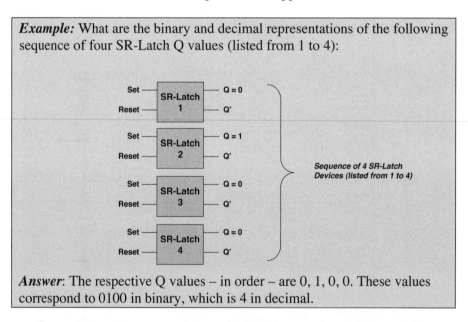

Answer: The respective Q values – in order – are 0, 1, 0, 0. These values
correspond to 0100 in binary, which is 4 in decimal.

Now that we understand what an SR-Latch is intended to do, we
can try to implement one using logic gates. The most obvious design of an
SR-latch can be built with a pair of NOR gates. You'll recall that a NOR
gate takes two inputs and produces an output of 1 only if both inputs are 0.
All other input combinations produce an output of 0. For the SR-Latch, the
two NOR gates are connected, and cross-connected, as follows:

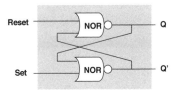

This arrangement of NOR gates includes two feedback loops where the output of one gate becomes an instantaneous input to another. If we examine the bottom NOR gate in the diagram, we can follow the feedback loop as follows:

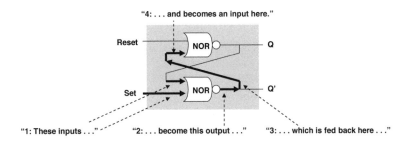

A key aspect of the feedback loop in this arrangement is the instantaneous aspect of the inputs and outputs. We can assume that at the instant the two inputs to the bottom NOR gate are set, the output is instantaneously determined, and that it is also immediately an input to the top NOR gate. This should be clear when you consider that these gates are implemented with connected electron flow, which – for all intents and purposes – can be viewed as instantaneous. The feedback loop for the top NOR gate can be shown as follows:

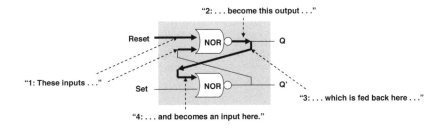

Understanding the full SR-Latch implementation will require that you analyze the operation of the gate inputs and outputs *very slowly and*

carefully in two steps. First, you start with the values that you assume to be present for Q and Q'. These become initial inputs to the NOR gates because of the feedback loops. Once you analyze the total input to the NOR gates, then you can figure out what the correct new output values are for Q and Q'.

Let's go through an example. Suppose that we start with Q = 0 and Q' = 1, and that we want to set Q to 1. We will assume that the values of the Reset and Set connections are both 0. We can also assume that some device or external entity is controlling the values of Reset and Set, and that the result of whatever is placed on Reset and Set, will determine the values of Q and Q'. The initial state of the SR-Latch is therefore as follows:

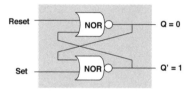

Now let's evaluate what happens when we make the Reset value 0 and the Set value 1. The initial output Q becomes input to the bottom NOR gate and the initial output Q' becomes input to the top NOR gate as follows:

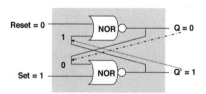

This causes the new values for Q and Q' to be 0 since NOR gates are only 1 when both inputs are 0. But then this new Q' becomes a new input to the top NOR gate. This causes the top NOR gate to now output a 1, which was the purpose of the Set operation in the first place. So the final configuration of the SR-latch is as follows:

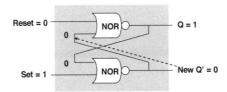

It is sometimes difficult for students to understand how gate combinations operate. Perhaps the only way to gain any type of understanding involves drawing the gate combination – in this case, the SR-Latch, and then setting up example combinations of inputs and outputs and tracing how the gate logic would change or not change the outputs. There is no magic to gaining insight here; you have to do the hard work of going through examples if you really want to understand how gate logic works.

7: Binary Adders

Mathematics are well and good but nature keeps dragging us around by the nose.

Albert Einstein

An SR-Latch is a *passive* device, because it accepts and stores the information it is given, without making changes. In contrast, every computer contains an *active* component known as a *central processing unit (CPU)*. Also referred to informally as the brain of a computer, the CPU performs operations on binary data in memory. For example, it can write information to memory; it can delete information from memory; it can make changes to information in memory; and so on.

The operation of a typical CPU in a modern computer is quite complex; but at the heart of a CPU is a set of simple arithmetic operations that can be demonstrated using logic gates. The *addition* operation is performed in a CPU using either a *half-adder* or a *full-adder*. A half adder takes two bits as input and produces a two-bit output which represents the sum of the two inputs. The truth table for a half-adder is as follows:

A	B	C	S
0	0	0	0
0	1	0	1
1	0	0	1
1	1	1	0

In the truth table, the two inputs are represented by A and B, and the two outputs are represented by C and S (S stands for *sum*, and C stands for *carry*). The addition is simple: $0 + 0 = 0$; $0 + 1 = 1$; $1 + 0 = 1$; and finally $1 + 1 = 10$. Thus, the carry bit is set only when 1 and 1 are being added.

A half-adder can be implemented using an AND gate and a device called an exclusive-OR gate (XOR). Let's first show the diagram and schematic for XOR (and note that the A, B, and C used here as variables in the truth table have nothing to do with their use as variables to designate two inputs and the carry output for adders):

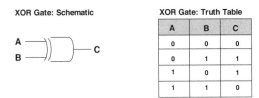

XOR Gate: Schematic

XOR Gate: Truth Table

A	B	C
0	0	0
0	1	1
1	0	1
1	1	0

XOR generates an output of 1 only when the two inputs are different. This explains its name: it's like an OR gate, but produces output 1 only if one of the inputs is exclusively 1. We can use this XOR function with an AND gate to create a simple half adder as follows:

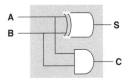

So let's examine the operation of this half-adder. In order to do so, we will have to examine some intermediate values since we are connecting outputs and inputs. Suppose that we start with A and B both set to 0:

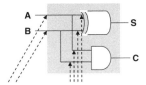

"If these two inputs are both 0 . . ."   *". . . then these four inputs are also 0."*

You can see from the diagram that when both A and B are 0, the four inputs to the two logic gates will all be 0. The result of these inputs being 0 is that the sum and carry values, S and C, must also be 0, as shown below:

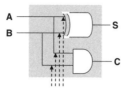

"If these four inputs are 0 ..."   "... then these two outputs are both 0."

If we set either A or B to be 1 (but not both), then we would expect that the result would be the sum value S equal to 1 and the carry value C equal to 0:

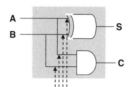

"If A is 1 and B is 0 ..."   "... then S is 1 and C is 0."

Finally, if both the A and B inputs are set to 1, then we would expect the values of the sum and carry outputs to also be 1:

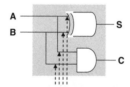

"If both A and B are 1 ..."   "... then S is 0 and C is 1."

Example: Show all possible combinations of inputs and outputs to the half adder:

Answer: Inputs to the half adder are A and B, and the outputs from the half adder are S and C. We can enumerate the possible combinations of inputs and outputs as follows:

• Inputs: A = 0, B = 0; Outputs: C = 0, S = 0
• Inputs: A = 0, B = 1; Outputs: C = 0, S = 1
• Inputs: A = 1, B = 0; Outputs: C = 0, S = 1
• Inputs: A = 1, B = 1; Outputs: C = 1, S = 1

While the half-adder is useful, it can only add two binary inputs. To add larger numbers, we will need a device that can be connected together with other similar devices to perform more complex operations. The *full adder,* shown schematically below, is just such a device:

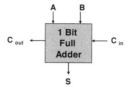

A full-adder takes two inputs A and B, just like a half-adder; but it also accepts an additional *carry* input, shown as C_{in}. The full-adder produces two outputs, C_{out} and S, not unlike the half-adder. The idea is that the carry output from one full-adder can be connected as input to a second full-adder device.

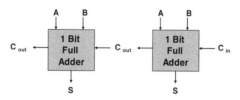

The result is that three binary inputs are considered in the full-adder: the A and B inputs to be added, as well as the carry value from any device that might be connected. If no devices are connected, then the carry value is 0.

Let's look briefly at the behavior of the full-adder in terms of the eight possible values of inputs for A, B, and C_{in}:

- <u>Inputs</u>: $C_{in} = 0$, $A = 0$, $B = 0$; <u>Outputs</u>: $C_{out} = 0$, $S = 0$
- <u>Inputs</u>: $C_{in} = 0$, $A = 0$, $B = 1$; <u>Outputs</u>: $C_{out} = 0$, $S = 1$
- <u>Inputs</u>: $C_{in} = 0$, $A = 1$, $B = 0$; <u>Outputs</u>: $C_{out} = 0$, $S = 1$
- <u>Inputs</u>: $C_{in} = 0$, $A = 1$, $B = 1$; <u>Outputs</u>: $C_{out} = 1$, $S = 0$
- <u>Inputs</u>: $C_{in} = 1$, $A = 0$, $B = 0$; <u>Outputs</u>: $C_{out} = 0$, $S = 1$
- <u>Inputs</u>: $C_{in} = 1$, $A = 0$, $B = 1$; <u>Outputs</u>: $C_{out} = 1$, $S = 0$
- <u>Inputs</u>: $C_{in} = 1$, $A = 1$, $B = 0$; <u>Outputs</u>: $C_{out} = 1$, $S = 0$
- <u>Inputs</u>: $C_{in} = 1$, $A = 1$, $B = 1$; <u>Outputs</u>: $C_{out} = 1$, $S = 1$

You can see that the addition operation is performed pretty much as you'd expect. For instance, 0 plus 0 plus a carry of 0 results in the two outputs being 0; alternatively, 1 plus 1 plus a carry of 1, produces the two outputs being 1.

Below is an implementation of a full-adder using one OR gate, two XOR gates, and two AND gates:

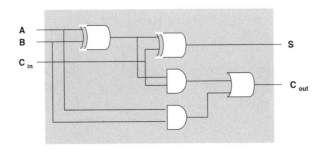

Rather than go through the complete analysis of this implementation, let's trace through a couple of examples. Suppose that A is 0, B is 0, and C_{in} is 0. The result you would expect would be for S to be 0 and C_{out} to be 0. So let's trace these values through the implementation starting with the three input values of 0:

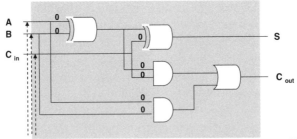

"If these three inputs are 0 ..."   "... then the seven inputs shown above are 0."

If we trace further, we can see that the XOR gate shown at the top of the diagram will produce an output of 0 as per its defined behavior. This 0 output thus becomes a second input to the other XOR gate at the top right of the diagram:

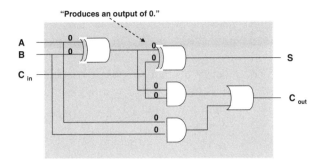

So now we can work through the outputs of the three gates in the middle of the full-adder implementation. As you can see below, their outputs are also all 0:

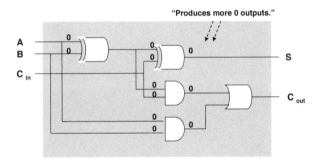

Finally, we can see that the output of the final OR gate must be 0 since its two inputs are 0. This results in the two final outputs to the full-adder being as expected:

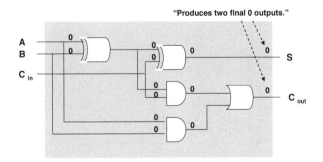

The full-adder is an important device because it shows how more complex systems can be built from smaller components. Computer scientists generally like this idea of constructing larger devices from smaller connected components. In fact, this basic concept, sometimes referred to as *composition*, is how massive systems like the Internet were conceived and built. You'll see this later when we begin to design software.

Spotlight: Charles Babbage

In the early 1800's, *Charles Babbage*, a somewhat gruff and eccentric mathematics professor from Cambridge University in England, invented what is now viewed by most historians as the first computer. His so-called *difference engine* was designed to create mathematical tables. Much of his work was funded by British Government, even though politicians at the time considered Babbage's work to be nonsense.

The difference engine had many of the properties of a modern computer. Data and programs were stored in a crude memory that was constructed mechanically from parts that Babbage and his assistant had to design and build from scratch. Like a modern computer, the engine had a central processor which he called a *mill* that would execute instructions. Like modern processors, it had an input/output procedure for users. A revised computer Babbage designed called the *analytical engine* used paper cards with punched holes that defined instructions and data.

One of Babbage's colleagues, a woman whose first name was *Ada,* would become the first person to write a useful program for his analytical engine. As a result, historians generally credit Ada with being the first computer programmer ever. Interestingly, in the 1980's, the United States Department of Defense designed a modern programming language, which they named Ada, in her honor. Unfortunately, the language did not generate sufficient interest to remain in use today – but both Babbage and Ada live on as the earliest pioneers of computer science.

8: Model of a Computer

*There is a computer disease that anybody who works with
computers knows about. It's a very serious disease and it
interferes completely with the work. The trouble with
computers is that you 'play' with them!*

Richard Feynman

The functionality of the gates and components examined so far can be
described in terms of binary input values being used to produce
some desired binary output value. Similarly, we will describe the
electronic devices used to construct computers in terms of how they
produce output values from input values:

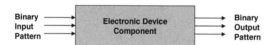

This concept of *inputs producing outputs* is the secret that makes
an electronic computer possible. Let's start our discussion of computers
with a simple model: Every computer can be thought of as having three
main components: (1) a *central processing unit* (CPU) that fetches and
executes special instructions, (2) an array of *memory* that is used to store
binary data and instructions, and (3) some method for a user to perform
input and output (I/O) operations into and out of the computer. These three
elements are shown in the following simple model of a computer:

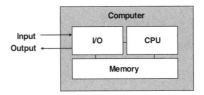

As you would expect, every computer you use at home and at school has these three components. For example, you provide *input* to a computer using a keyboard or storage device (like a compact disc); you obtain *output* from a computer through a flat screen or printer; you store data inside the *memory* of a computer or on a removable component like a memory stick; and your computer has a *central processing unit* or *CPU* that does the computational work. These are the basic functions of any computer.

Our earlier discussions were intended to give you a basic idea of the underlying technology used in these three components of a computer. You saw, for example, binary information being added using logic gates. Although this is a simple computation, it does give you a *general idea* of how logic components can perform useful work as in a CPU. You also saw how a device called an SR-latch could be used to store binary data. This additionally gives you a *general idea* of how information can be stored in a computer memory.

Example: Which of the following devices do you think could be interpreted reasonably as a computer?

  a) Your smart phone
  b) The toaster in your kitchen
  c) Your family car

Answer: Certainly your smart phone can be interpreted as a computer; it has clear input mechanisms, it stores and processes information, and it provides output. The toaster in your kitchen does not easily qualify as a computer since it does not process or store information (although any timer or clock on the toaster might have some computer-like functions). Your family car is not primarily a computer since its main function is to transport people; but many of the devices in a car, including the entertainment system, could reasonably be interpreted as computers. Future cars will be increasingly designed to include and rely upon computers for their operation, safety, and usage.

Now let's introduce a more detailed view of the operation of a computer. You will recall that memory consists of a long array of binary information. There are two types of binary information in memory: (1) *instructions* that direct the CPU to perform some useful operation, and (2) *data*, perhaps input from some user that is used by the CPU when it executes stored instructions. Usually, instructions are stored in one portion of memory, and data is stored in another portion. Here is a view of how instructions and data might typically be partitioned in a computer memory:

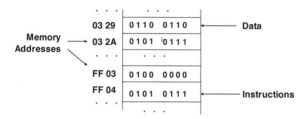

Each "storage slot" in memory, sometimes referred to as a *memory word*, is numbered with a so-called memory *address*. In the diagram above, we picked arbitrary hexadecimal numbers to show the memory addresses which are shown to include *eight-bit* memory words. This is important because computer system designers must decide how long the words in memory must be. Many modern computers operate on 32-bit words.

Example: What is the decimal value of the eight-bit memory word stored in address FF03 in the previous diagram?

Answer: Looking at that address, we can see that the binary number 0100 0000 is stored in the memory address starting at FF03. Converting this number to its decimal representation produces a value of 64.

The CPU interacts with memory using something called a *fetch-execute cycle*. In order for the fetch-execute cycle to work, a temporary binary storage location located inside the CPU called a *program counter* is set to contain the address in memory of the next instruction the CPU must execute. Here is the two-step process involved in the cycle:

Step 0: Fetch. The CPU fetches the instruction at the memory address specified in the program counter.

Step 1: Execute. The CPU executes that instruction and the program counter is incremented to the next memory address.

If you're wondering how a CPU can *fetch* something, just imagine that it points its inputs to the location of memory specified in the program counter. That binary memory pattern then causes outputs to occur in the CPU, which might be adding, storing, or whatever.

As we look more closely at computer operations in the coming chapters, you'll see that while CPUs can do much more than just adding and storing, they really do not perform highly complex operations. Instead, small and simple operations in the CPU are used as building blocks for creating more complicated functions like the ones you use on your computer every day.

The fetch-execute cycle for a CPU and memory in a computer can be depicted as follows:

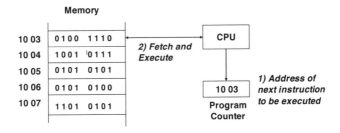

In the diagram above, after the instruction is executed, the program counter will be incremented from 10 03 to 10 04, and the CPU will execute that instruction next. This is how computers continually execute instructions.

Let's step through a couple of fetch-execute cycles more carefully to see how that affected values change in each step. Let's start with the diagram shown below:

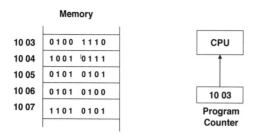

In the diagram above, we show a portion of memory with eight-bit word instructions, starting at memory address 1003. The Program Counter is pointing at 1003, so this starts the cycle at this location.

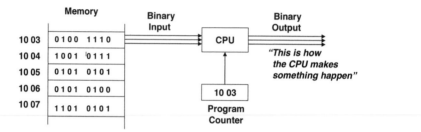

As you can see in the diagram above, when the Program Counter is pointed at 1003, the CPU "points to" or "fetches" the memory word at location 1003 and uses this binary information as input. Just as we described in the beginning of the chapter, the CPU uses this input to create a corresponding output to occur. We refer to this input and output process for a CPU as *instruction execution.*

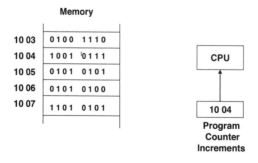

Once an instruction has been executed, the Program Counter is incremented to the next memory location, as shown in the diagram above.

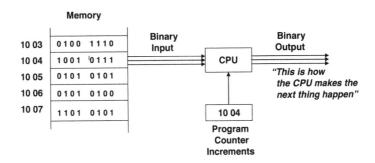

Finally, the Program Counter "points" to or *fetches* the next instruction at the location now pointed to by the Program Counter. This fetch-execute cycle is the essence of computer operations, and enables everything we do with computers in our lives. It is truly the secret to how a computer can operate automatically.

9: CPU Design

Anyone can build a fast CPU. The trick is to build a fast system.

Seymour Cray

tudents often wonder how a *central processing unit* (*CPU*) can *execute* instructions. This is particularly true with respect to the fetch-execute cycle. Students often wonder how a CPU can understand what computer instructions are designed to do. The answer lies in how binary numbers become input to a device and how that device in turn processes them into outputs.

You will recall, for example, that we previously provided binary numbers as input to an adder, which in turn produced their sum as output. We could have interpreted this as the device 'executing' or 'understanding' an addition instruction. It's not that the device has any special intelligence or knowledge of the instruction, but rather that the device has been designed to operate on the binary input in a specific way.

A CPU is much more complicated than a simple adder, but it turns out that it can be decomposed into several smaller functions, each of which performs a logical operation. Three of the most important operations that will be required in a CPU include the following:

- *Input*: This involves obtaining the binary instruction presented as input to the CPU over the wires used for such input. Every CPU will have its own special set of instructions that it can use.
- *Instruction Execution*: This involves the decoding and performance of whatever operation is associated with the instruction. This is the heart of the CPU operation and will include functions such as arithmetic processing (e.g., addition).
- *Input/Output*: This involves storing and retrieving information from memory that might be necessary for the instruction. This is

also done using special wires that are connected to the rest of the computer system.

Thus, at the highest level, a typical CPU architecture can be viewed as having the following representation:

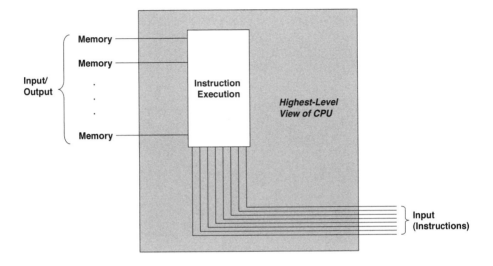

Now let's use this high level representation to show how the inside of a typical CPU is organized in more detail. In particular, we will look inside the component labeled in the diagram above as *Instruction Execution*. As you might guess, it contains a variety of more specific and detailed electronic components, each of which performs a very specific task. The primary internal components of the instruction execution portion of a CPU are as follows:

- *Instruction Register*: This is where a fetched instruction is temporarily held as it is being executed. It must be designed to have sufficient size to house any instruction.
- *Instruction Decoder*: This is the complex logic used to decode a computer instruction into a set of operational steps. You can think of this as defining the language of the CPU.
- *Arithmetic Logic Unit*: This the computer logic component used to perform arithmetic computations. Even in a complex computer system, basic arithmetic is often at the base of most operations.

- *Registers*: These are temporary memory slots the CPU uses for keeping information. In fact, the term *register* is often used synonymously with the term *memory slot*. One of the registers in a CPU is the *accumulator*. Another CPU register is a *buffer* for input instructions. Other useful CPU registers include the *X register* and the *Y register*.
- *Buses*: These are the data connections between elements inside the computer, almost like tiny little networks. Buses generally come in multiples of eight bits to complement the use of binary arithmetic in operations.

CPUs include many more components than this; for example, we previously referenced a component known as a *program counter*. But the ones listed above will be sufficient and useful for our present discussion. Their basic organization and interconnection is shown in the diagram below:

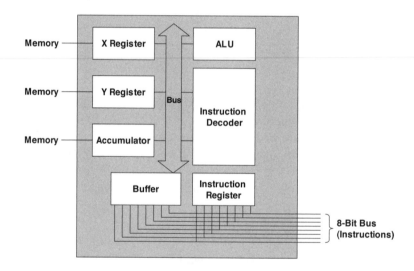

In the diagram, you can see that instructions enter the CPU on a *bus*, shown above as having eight bits. The instruction becomes input to an *instruction register*, which then feeds that input to an *instruction decoder*. The decoder knows all of the instructions and produces output, usually to the registers, based on what the instruction was designed to do. A bus is also included for passing information between the various registers.

Let's look more closely at this logical flow in a step-by-step manner. The first step involves an instruction being presented to the CPU from the 8-bit bus input. The instruction goes directly into the instruction register.

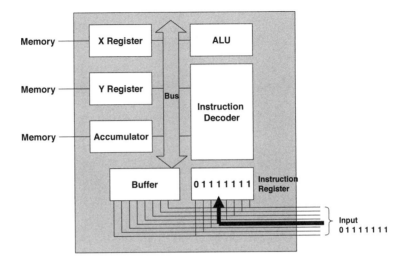

The instruction register is just an electronic device that is designed to perform its one basic function, which is storing the information presented as an instruction to the CPU. Once the instruction register has the information, it is also true that the buffer register holds the information as well. From this buffer, the information is presented to the instruction decoder, which is designed to accept the instruction and determine the task that is required.

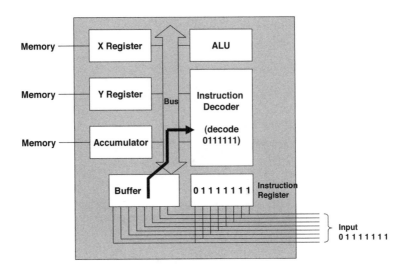

The instruction decoder is designed to utilize the various registers of the CPU to perform its basic functions. These registers are often used to store and retain interim results when some calculation is being done by the ALU.

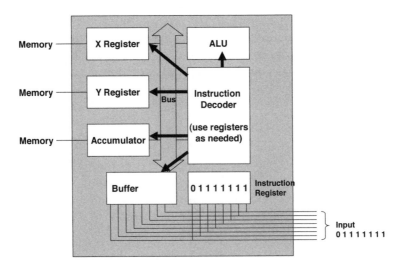

Finally, the interactions between the CPU and the rest of the computer, which is generally the memory slots of the computer, will be performed through registers in the CPU.

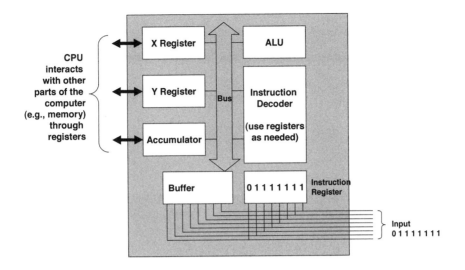

You will soon see that CPU instructions tend to be designed to perform simple computational tasks on memory or registers. Some examples of the simple tasks performed in typical sorts of CPU instructions include the following:

- *Example Instructional Task*: Put a value in the X register.
- *Example Instructional Task*: Move a value from the accumulator to memory.
- *Example Instructional Task*: Grab a value in memory and move to the Y register.

Every CPU is designed with its own instructions, which are referred to collectively as the *instruction set* for that CPU. Certain types of Apple computers, for example, will have one CPU and instruction set, whereas certain types of IBM computers will have a different CPU and instruction set. This might help you understand why games for one type of computer do not always run on another type of computer.

As we continue our discussion, you'll soon see how we can string instructions together for a CPU into more complex objects that will be called *computer programs*, or even more simply as *computer software*.

10: Loading and Storing

There is a constant need for new systems and new software.

Marc Andreassen

At the simplest level, CPU instructions are nothing more than sequences of binary digits which are interpreted by the CPU to perform a specific task. These binary instructions are referred to by computer scientists as *machine language instructions*. To make things simpler for human beings, however, each machine language instruction is associated with a readable and meaningful name that is descriptive of its task.

Let's introduce an instruction LDX (pronounced 'load X') that performs the following task: It loads some designated numeric value into the X register. For example, to load hexadecimal value 01 into the X register, the instruction would look like this:

The LDX part of this instruction is referred to as the *opcode*, and the 01 is referred to as the *operand*. It is important to understand that operands can be specified in different ways. For instance, the operand might be a specific value, such as the 01 value shown above in the LDX example. Alternatively, the operand could refer to the contents of some designated memory location or register. As we introduce example instructions below, we will differentiate between these options using different syntax.

Since instructions and data are stored as 0's and 1's, the CPU designer would assign a binary code to the LDX instruction (as the machine language representation). So, for example, the code for LDX might be, say, 0111 1000.[1] Thus, the instruction LDX 01 would look like this in memory:

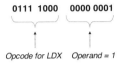

The CPU instruction register would accept the binary input and perform the corresponding load operation. In this case, what happens is that 01 (shown as 0000 0001)[2] would be placed into the X register. The diagram below shows the result of the LDX operation:

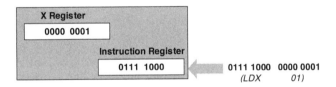

Example: Using the LDX, write an instruction that clears the X register.

Answer: The use of the term 'clear" implies writing a sequence of 0's. The LDX instruction would thus simply take all zeroes as the operand to perform this task. Hence, the instruction would be LDX 0000 0000. This can be shortened to LDX 00, or even LDX 0.

A second instruction, that we will call STX (pronounced 'store X') will store the value of the X register in the memory location specified in the operand of the instruction. For example, the instruction STX #4B will store the value of the X register into memory location 4B. Note that we use the # sign in the operand to show that we're referring to the memory

---

[1] Note that this machine language representation is just a hypothetical example. The code 0111 1000 is just a made up binary sequence to illustrate the concept. Obviously, in a real CPU, this code would be carefully designed and specified.

[2] Note that throughout this book, we do not draw distinction between numbers written as 01, 001, 0001, and so on. Leading zeroes are shown in the context of the discussion to make things easier to understand.

location 4B, rather than the numeric value 4B. Different CPU designers will specify memory in their operands in different ways.

Also, just as with the LDX instruction, the CPU designers would assign a binary code to the STX opcode. In spite of our casual reference to this assignment, computer system designers must take this task of assigning codes seriously. In space applications, for example, spurious one bit changes to memory are possible as a result of radiation in outer space; hence, instructions must be designed so that one bit changes to an instruction will not produce some other instruction, perhaps with disastrous consequences. As you would guess, designers of computer systems in spacecrafts figured this one out the hard way.

Anyway, let's assume, for our example that the binary code for the STX instruction with a memory address in the operand is 0001 0010 which is 12 in hexadecimal. The diagram below shows the result of the operation if the hexadecimal value 01 is in the X register:

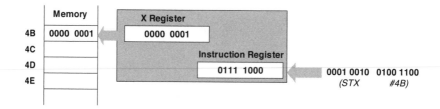

Example: Using the STX, write an instruction that puts the value of the X register into memory location 5E.

Answer: The STX instruction would use #5E as the operand to perform this task. Hence, the instruction would be STX #0000 005E, which can be shortened to STX #5E.

Using these two simple operations, LDX and STX, we can write out our first simple *computer program*. Since LDX and STX are so simple, we can't do too much in our first program, but we can illustrate the basic idea of how we'll be putting instructions together into more complex programs later. Our example will also show how information is moved about between registers and memory by computer software. Let's call our sample program *Clear Memory Location FF*:

-- Program Name: Clear Memory Location FF:

```
LDX  00      -- Loads value 00 into the X register
STX  #FF     -- Stores contents X register into location FF
```

The effect of the program can be shown through the value of the X register before the program runs, and then also after the program runs. The 'before value' is referred to by computer scientists as a *precondition*, and the 'after value' as a *postcondition*. Research has been done be computer scientists about how one might mathematically derive program code from pre and post-conditions. This is not possible today for anything but the simplest code, but it might be useful for programmers in the future. Below we show the pre and post-conditions for our trivial example program above.

-- Pre: X register and location FF: unspecified values

```
LDX  00      -- Loads 00 into the X register
STX  #FF     -- Stores value X register into location FF
```

-- Post: X register and location FF: contain value 00

In all computer programs, some sort of language convention is used to designate a so-called *comment* that is not considered part of the program. In the example above, the convention involves two line dashes, followed by a comment, and completed by the end of the line. Sometimes, languages include the convention of enclosing the start and end of a comment with some designation, such as shown below:

/* here is a comment */

Comments are intended to help human beings understand what's going on in a program, but are totally ignored by any automation or other systems that are using the program. This is an especially important technique since most professional programmers spend their time doing *maintenance* of existing programs, rather than design of new programs. So computer program *readability* has always been an important consideration in computer science.

It's obvious, but worth noting that computer programs like the one above are referred to collectively as *software*. The software that runs on your computer is a zillion times more complicated then our sample program; but the basic concept of stringing related instructions together into a program with attention to maintenance and readability remains the same.

11: Jumping Logic

If you want to go somewhere, goto is the best way to get there.

Ken Thompson

The computer programs we wrote in the previous chapters had instructions that were executed in the order in which they were listed from top to bottom. You'll recall that one of the programs looked and executed as follows:

Execute This Instruction First ⸺⸺⸺▶ **LDX 00**   *Direction of the*
Execute This Instruction Second ⸺⸺▶ **STX #4B**   *Execution Flow*
And so on . . .

What is happening is that in the CPU, a special internal register called a *program counter* is set with the address of the instruction to be executed. It's a pointer to the location in memory of the next instruction the CPU should be prepared to run. If you were to freeze a computer at some instant and look inside the CPU, you'd see that the value of the program counter would contain the memory location of the instruction the CPU is executing (or about to). After an instruction is executed, the program counter is *incremented* to the next memory location ('incrementing' means counting upward).

An example will help to illustrate. Let's assume that the program counter in a CPU contains the value of hexadecimal 39. This implies that the CPU should execute the instruction located in that memory slot. If the program from our previous discussion referenced above was located beginning at memory location 39 where the LDX 00 is located, then the *state* of the CPU at that instant would look as follows:

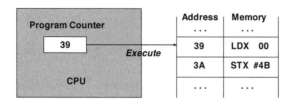

Since the LDX 00 instruction is located at address 39, the CPU would execute that instruction. After the LDX 00 instruction was executed, the program counter would then be incremented to the next memory location, which is hexadecimal 3A.

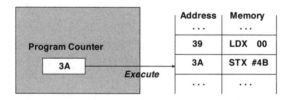

Now that the program counter has been incremented to 3A, the STX #4B instruction stored in that memory location will be executed:

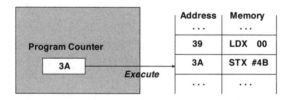

As you can see, the normal program flow goes from one instruction, to the next instruction in memory, to the next one, and so on. Technically, this progression would continue on forever in a computer until the machine is turned off since there is often no notion in a CPU of the fetch-execute cycle ever stopping.

Example: If memory locations 20, 21, 22, and 23 contain successive instructions of a program, and the program counter contains the value 20, describe one way for the program counter to eventually become set to the instruction in memory location 23?

Answer: One way would be for the program counter to increment once to 21, a second time to 22, and then a third time to get to the instruction in memory location 23. This execution sequence corresponds to the program executing the successive instructions. As you will soon see, however, the program counter can be set arbitrarily by computer programs, so there are infinitely many different ways for the program counter to find its way to memory location 23.

To provide more control for the programmer, however, a special instruction called *JMP* (pronounced 'jump) is included in the instruction set of every CPU. It causes the program counter to be changed to whatever the programmer desires, rather than just the location of the next instruction in memory. When executed, JMP sets the program counter to the memory address specified in the JMP operand.

Let's look at a simple example. Suppose that three instructions of a program being executed are stored in memory locations 20, 21, and 22. Suppose further that the program counter holds value 20 and is read to execute the instruction in that memory location which happens to be the JMP instruction. Furthermore, the operand in the JMP instruction is set to jump to location 22. Here is how things look to start:

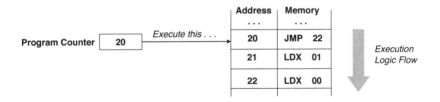

Since the instruction being executed at location 20 is a JMP instruction to location 22, the program counter is incremented to the value of 22. This implies that the instruction at location 21 is skipped over. The result is that the LDX 00 instruction would be the next one to be executed:

Address	Memory	
. . .	. . .	
20	JMP	22
21	LDX	01
22	LDX	00

Now execute this

Program Counter 22

Execution Logic Flow

Here's another example showing the first three instructions of a program being executed. In this one, we see the presumed logical flow of the first three steps. First, the LDX 00 instruction is executed; then the STX #4B instruction is executed; and then the JMP #39 instruction is executed:

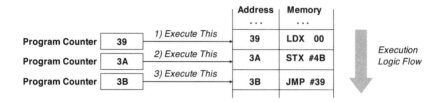

After the JMP instruction is executed, the program counter is set to the operand value of hexadecimal 39. This is shown below:

			Address	Memory	
			...	...	
Program Counter	39	Execute Here Again	39	LDX 00	
			3A	STX #4B	Jump
					Execute
			3B	JMP #39	Logic

Computer programmers refer to this type of logic as a *program loop*, because the program flow loops back to an earlier address. Thus, the JMP instruction allows more complex and effective programs to be written. Programmers must be careful with JMP, however, because a program written with too many loops and skips can easily become a tangled mess.

For example, the program written above that jumps up to memory location 39 will go on over and over, never ending, in a condition known as an infinite loop. The programmer might want this functionality for some reason (as we will examine in the next chapter), but in most cases, infinite loops are errors that need to be either prevented from occurring in the first place, or detected and removed from a program.

This is done via *software testing*. Most computer scientists know that testing is good at finding the presence of errors, but inadequate at ensuring their avoidance. For example, a program might contain obscure functionality that could only be known by reading the code. Testing might never, ever uncover such functionality. As a result, careful analysis of one's software during its design and development is a much more effective approach toward correct code than performing a lot of testing after it has been written.

12: Branching Logic

When you arrive at a fork in the road, take it.

Yogi Berra

Recall from the previous chapter that the JMP instruction was designed to adjust the value of the program counter. The execution flow for a loop program using JMP, one that simply loads hexadecimal 45 into the X register and then stores that value into memory location 23, and then goes on forever and ever, might look as follows:

```
34    LDX    45
      STX    #23
      JMP    #34
```

The flow starts with the first instruction, which is labeled as being located in memory location #34. The flow then moves to the second instruction, then moves to the third instruction, then goes back to the first instruction, and so on. This example program will continually repeat these operations, over and over, without ever ending. This repeat condition, as mentioned above, is called an *infinite loop*.

Example: Create a simple set of driving instructions that would result in an infinite loop.

Answer: Suppose that we wish to create driving instructions to some destination located several blocks away and only reachable by turning immediately left. The following instructions would result in the car entering an infinite loop:

59

Step 1: If location Y is immediately adjacent to your car, then you are finished.
Step 2: Otherwise, make a right turn and go to end of block.
Step 3: Repeat Step 1.

It should be obvious by reading these instructions that location Y will never be adjacent to your car, and that you will end up going around and around the block forever.

It is worth mentioning again that not all infinite loops like the one above are bad. Certainly, a loop that continually writes the same value to a memory location seems useless; but if an infinite loop was designed to perform some repeat operation such as checking status of an indicator and then displaying the value, that would seem much more useful.

Example: Create a simple set of "traffic light instructions" that would result in an infinite loop.

Answer: The following set of instructions and associated loop would be typical for many simple traffic lights:

Step 1: Set light to green and wait 30 seconds.
Step 2: Set light to yellow and wait 5 seconds.
Step 3: Set light to red and wait 30 seconds.
Step 4: Repeat Step 1.

It should be obvious by reading these instructions that the traffic light operates in an infinite loop, which is precisely the desired intent.

To increase control of execution flow and to avoid *unwanted* infinite loops, an instruction called BRX (pronounced 'branch X') is used to change or branch to the value of the program counter. BRX causes a branch to occur only if the value in the X register is *not* zero. Here are two sample BRX program traces:

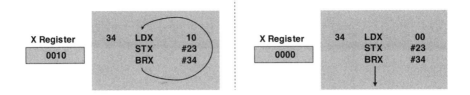

In the first (left) case, the X register has a non-zero value, so the BRX instruction causes execution flow to return up to the instruction at address 34. This corresponds to another unwanted infinite loop. In the second (right) case, the X register has a zero value, so the BRX instruction causes execution to continue on past the loop to whatever instruction follows the BRX. Computer scientists refer to this structure as a *conditional loop*, and they further refer to the X register being zero as the *exit condition* for the loop.

Before we use branching logic and conditional loops to write some more interesting programs, let's introduce three new instructions on the X and Y registers:

INY	*-- Adds one to the value stored in the Y register*
DEX	*-- Subtracts one from value stored in X register*
LDY nn	*-- Loads the hex value nn into the Y register*

So let's write a simple program using BRX and the three instructions we've just introduced. Our example will do nothing more than to count up to 5 in the Y register, using the X register as a helpful index:

-- Program Name: Count to 05 in Y Register:

	LDX	05	-- Loads hexadecimal 05 into X register
	LDY	00	-- Loads hexadecimal 00 into Y register
2D	INY		-- Increments value in Y register by 1
	DEX		-- Decrements value in X register by 1
	BRX	2D	-- Jumps to location 2D unless X register is 0

It helps to mentally execute each instruction, writing down the values of the X and Y registers each time the instructions are executed:

- *LDX and LDY*: After these instructions are executed, the X register holds 5, and the Y register holds 0. Computer scientists often refer to the preliminary setting of any registers as their *initialization*.

  | X Register | 05 | | Y Register | 00 |

- *INY and DEX*: The INY instruction is said to be *labeled*, which means that its address (2D) is specifically shown in the program. The other instructions are located in memory but not labeled. INY simply adds 1 to the Y register. Similarly, the DEX instruction subtracts 1 from the X register.

  | X Register | 04 | | Y Register | 01 |

- *BRX*: When BRX is reached the first time, the X register holds 4, and the Y register holds 1. Since the value in the X register is not 0, the BRX instruction will jump the execution flow to memory address 2D.
- *Loop Termination:* Eventually, the X register decrements down to 0 and the Y register increments up to 5. When this occurs, the BRX will not jump back up to the instruction at 2D and the loop will be said to have *conditionally terminated*.

An important method for examining and understanding a program such as the one written above involves defining the entrance and exit conditions that are desired for that program. This gives the programmer a means for *testing* whether the program logic is working as expected. In fact, most programmers create *test plans* that perform this type of analysis – checking whether a desired condition is met at a given point in the program flow.

13: Stack PUSH and POP

People who are more than casually interested in computers should have at least some idea of what the underlying hardware is like. Otherwise, the programs they write will be pretty weird.

Donald Knuth

A *stack* is like an open box where plates are stacked on top of each other. In a computer, a stack is a block of contiguous memory locations into which data can be placed or removed. Placing data onto a stack is called *pushing* and removing data from the stack is called *popping*. Obviously, pushing data onto a stack involves placing it on top of the existing data, and popping data from a stack involves removing from the top of the stack.

The stack is one of the most fundamental and important data structure concepts in all of computing, since it is the basis for a large number of procedural operations required in a computer system. As such, the stack concept comes up over and over again in the study of computer science.

Example: Show how a stack of five dinner plates can be arranged into a stack and associated with push and pop operations.

Answer: The stack of five plates can be pushed and popped as shown in the example below.

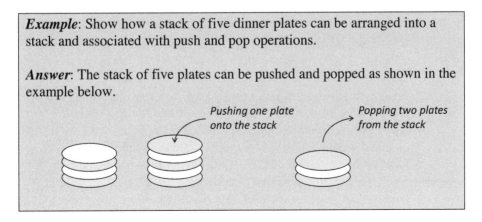

Pushing one plate onto the stack

Popping two plates from the stack

In the context of computer systems, two instructions associated with a stack are the PUSH instruction, which places data onto the top of the stack, and the POP instruction which removes the top element of the stack and places it into the accumulator. Below is a visual depiction of PUSH and POP in memory:

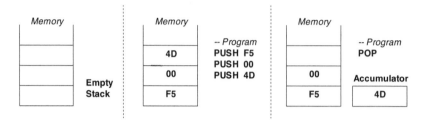

In the first (leftmost) panel above, we see an empty block of memory addresses reserved for use as a stack. In the second (middle) panel, we see the result of three consecutive PUSH operations. You can see the stack filling up just as a stack of dishes would fill up in a box. In the third (rightmost) panel, we see the result of one POP operation, where the top element of the stack is removed and placed into the accumulator register.

The operation of a stack has a so-called *last-in, first-out* (LIFO) type function for the PUSH and POP instructions. We say this because the last data pushed to the stack will always be the first data popped. It's also worth noting that computer hackers love to try to *overflow* stacks in software by pushing more data than they can hold. The result is a stack overflow, which causes the software, and sometimes the entire computer, to go haywire. Let's now introduce four instructions that will help us write a useful program.

- *STA*: This instruction stores the accumulator value into a memory location. An example would be STA #32 which stores the accumulator into the memory location hexadecimal 32.
- *SAD*: This instruction POPs the top two values of the stack, adds them together, and then places the result into the accumulator.
- *BRA*: This instruction branches to a specified memory location. An example would be BRA #56, which branches to the memory location hexadecimal 56 only if the value of the accumulator is 0.
- *NOP*: This instruction does nothing more than move the program counter along. It is often used as a placeholder in a program.

Using these new instructions, we can write a program that demonstrates stacks, and uses the new instructions. The program will add two values from the stack and test whether the result is zero:

```
           -- Program Name: Add two pushed values and then test for 0 result

           PUSH   02      -- Pushes value 02 onto the stack
           PUSH   04      -- Pushes value 04 onto the stack
           SAD            -- POPs twice and places sum in accumulator
           BRA   #33      -- Jumps to location 33 if the accumulator is 0
           JMP   #35      -- Jumps over address 33 to address 35
      33   NOP            -- Program gets here if the added value is zero
      35   NOP            -- Program continues from here
```

So let's work through the execution:

- *PUSH Instructions*: The first two PUSH instructions result in 04 and 02 being placed onto the stack. The 04 value will be on top.
- *SAD Instruction*: This POPs the 02 and 04 and adds them, resulting in a 06 being placed into the accumulator.
- *BRA #33*: This causes a branch if the accumulator value is 0. In this example, the value is 06, so the program counter will just move to the next instruction.
- *JMP #35*: The program will jump over the instruction at address 33, because the value in the accumulator is not 0.

Example: Write a program that pushes four zero values onto a stack, and then pops two of them off.

Answer: The simplest program could be written as follows:

```
           PUSH 00        -- Pushes value 00 onto the stack
           PUSH 00
           PUSH 00
           PUSH 00
           POP            -- Pops the stack
           POP            -- Pops the stack
```

Even though our programs thus far have been quite simple, and don't really perform much in terms of useful or interesting computation, you should be getting somewhat comfortable now with writing down simple sequences of instructions based on a task you're trying to accomplish. This process of creating programs is referred to by computer scientists as *software development.*

Spotlight: Grace Hopper

In 1934, *Grace Murray Hopper* received the Ph.D. degree in mathematics from Yale University. She soon embarked on a distinguished career in computer science, forging new ground in many important areas and serving as a role model for decades of women interested in math and science. During her career, she served as a computer science educator, engineer, scientist, and member of the US Naval Reserve.

One of Grace Hopper's major contributions during her career was the development of the first *compiler*. She is also generally credited with coining the term "bug" in the context of computers. She was working on a computer called the Mark II at Harvard University in 1945, when she located a moth that was stuck inside one of the computer relays. Removing the moth was thus dubbed by Ms. Hopper *debugging* the machine, a term still used by computer scientists today.

Historians have come to recognize the wonderful contributions made by Grace Hopper to computer science, and especially to young people in computing. The Association for Computing Machinery (ACM) has established an award called the *Grace Murray Hopper Award for Outstanding Young Computer Professionals* which they've been awarding to deserving young computer scientists since 1971. Ms. Hopper passed away in 1992 and was laid to rest in Arlington National Cemetery.

14: Visual Display

Above all else, shown the data.

Edward Tufte

Everyone knows that computers provide output for humans on *visual displays*. An example visual display is the flat screen connected to your PC. The simplest type of visual output device is known as a *seven segment display*. It displays a single decimal digit from 0 to 9 as shown below:

A seven segment display is controlled by a computer program through a physical connection on the back of the display called an *interface*. This interface accepts binary numbers as inputs. Each of the segments in the display (denoted by t, u, v, w, x, y, and z above) is controlled by one bit of the input to the interface.

Suppose, for example, that the first bit in the input (rightmost binary digit) turns on the t segment in the display. If we assume that the computer doing the controlling has eight bit words, then the following input would turn on the t segment:

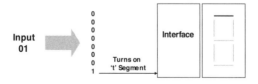

Let's suppose further that the second bit (the next-to-rightmost binary digit) turns on the u segment as follows:

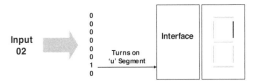

These examples are not that useful, because the t and u segments do not represent recognizable decimal digits. If we combine inputs, however, then we *can* create recognizable output. Suppose, for example, that the third bit will turn on the v segment. We could therefore display a decimal 1 by providing input as follows:

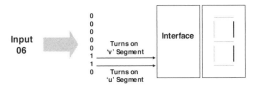

Following this logic, we can build a so-called *conversion table* that will show the input values that correspond to each of the decimal digits that can be displayed on the display device.

Digit	Code
0	3F
1	06
2	5B
3	4F
4	66
5	6D
6	7D
7	07
8	7F
9	6F

From the conversion table, we can see that an input of 7F will cause a decimal 8 to be displayed. Similarly, we can see that an input of 6F will cause a decimal digit 9 to be displayed. Note that since 6F is binary 01101111, the first (t), second (u), third (v), fourth (w), sixth (y), and seventh (z) segments are illuminated. Only the fifth (x) segment is not turned on. So a decimal 9 looks like this:

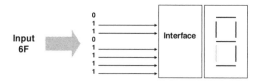

If you connect multiple seven segment displays together, then you can display numbers with multiple digits. Modern devices, such as flat screens, obviously use much more complex technology. But the basic notion is the same: Binary input is used to control what humans see on visual display screens.

If we connect a computer to a seven-segment display device, the set-up would look as follows:

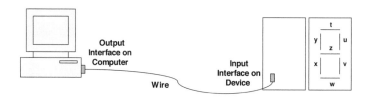

Let's assume that the output interface on the computer is capable of allowing eight-bit outputs to be sent from the computer, along the wire, to some connected device. We can assume further that the input interface on the device is capable of accepting eight-bit inputs, via a wired connection, from whatever computer or system is at the other end.

A computer can send data along a wire because the output interface on the computer is directly connected to a specific memory location. This is called *memory-mapped output*. So, for example, let's suppose that memory location FF is directly connected to the output interface. This can be depicted as follows:

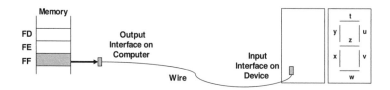

What this means is that if we load a specific value, say, 07 to memory location FF, then that value will instantaneously travel along the wire and become input to the device. We know from the conversion table in the previous discussion that 07 corresponds to the decimal digit 7. So the scenario of *writing* a 7 to the display would look like this:

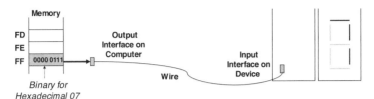

Note that if we try to depict hexadecimal values in the display, then we'll have trouble. The symbol for B looks the same as the symbol for 8; the symbol for D looks the same as the symbol for 0; and so on. So, we'll stick to only displaying decimal 0 through 9. In addition, note that the highest bit (leftmost binary digit) in the output word is not used. This is because there are only seven segments in the display, so we don't need all eight bits in the output word.

Let's now create a simple program to write values in memory to the display. Before we do, however, we need to introduce a version of the LDA (Load Accumulator) instruction that reads from memory, and version of the STA instruction that will copy the contents of the accumulator into memory:

- *LDA #nn*: This instruction reads the contents of memory location nn and places the value in the accumulator.
- *STA #nn*: This instruction stores the contents of the accumulator into memory location nn

Below is a program that reads the value of a memory location and writes it to the display, assuming that the memory location #FF is memory mapped to the display interface.

-- Program Name: Display decimal value in memory location 00

LDA   #00   -- Loads value of location 00 into the accumulator
STA   #FF   -- Stores value of accumulator into location FF

One program note is that if the memory location in FF is loaded with a value other than a valid one from the conversion table for this device, then things will go haywire. Programmers must exercise due care in avoiding such situations. Computer scientists refer to these errors as *bugs*.

A famous and influential computer scientist from Stanford University named Donald Knuth once wrote a long technical report summarizing all the bugs that he caused in a text formatting computer program that he created. He did this to help other programmers learn from his own mistakes.

15: Interrupts

The finest pieces of software are those where one individual has a complete sense of exactly how the program works.

Bill Gates

Students know they cannot interrupt a teacher, but that a teacher can interrupt them. The reason for this lies in a concept known as *prioritization*. Since teachers have higher *priority* than students, they can override students, but since students have lower priority, they cannot override teachers. Whether teachers can override other teachers, or whether students can override other students, is a local decision.

Let's relate this to computer science. Suppose that instructions are being executed normally by the CPU, when suddenly, some high priority event occurs elsewhere on the computer. For example, maybe the battery has run dangerously low on a laptop, and all work will be lost if the user is not prompted to save everything immediately. This is clearly a high priority event and requires attention.

In such a case, computers generate signals called *interrupts* that will stop the flow of an executing computer and transfer execution flow to a special program called an *interrupt handler*. The diagram below shows an interrupt being sent from a battery monitor to the CPU so that the user can take immediate action:

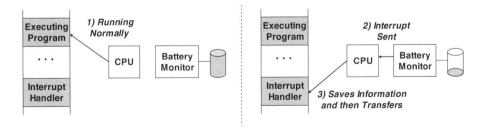

73

On the left side of the diagram, the CPU is shown running normally with the battery level full. On the right side, however, an interrupt causes execution flow to point to an interrupt handler because, as you can see, the battery level has run dangerously low.

Most computers have at least two levels of interrupt handling based on priority. The first level is usually referred to as a *non-maskable interrupt*. In this case, the urgency of the interrupt is so high that action must be taken immediately with no delay. Power management interrupts are usually in this category. The designers of the computer system will make the determination as to which types of events are considered non-maskable.

A second level involves maskable interrupts in which the program acknowledges the interrupt, but first finishes the immediate task at hand before turning control to the interrupt handler. Some computers process keyboard input this way. For example, when a key is depressed, a maskable interrupt is generated, and the CPU completes its task, stores its state, and processes the user input from the keyboard.

An interrupt is handled via an input line to *interrupt logic* in the CPU. The interrupt logic is always ready and waiting for a signal that something of high priority requires immediate attention. Below is the interrupt logic added to our CPU model:

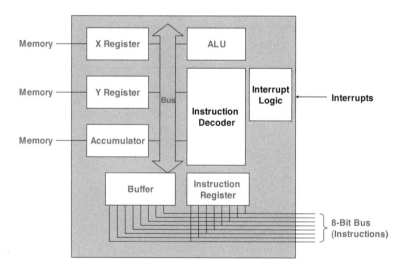

When an interrupt is received, the CPU will first save the current *state* of the executing program. This involves saving the memory location of the program counter, the values in the X and Y registers, the values in the accumulator, and any other relevant buffered or stored information. It does this, usually, by pushing these values onto a stack as shown below.

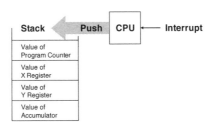

Once the interrupt handler has completed, execution flow is returned to the original program by popping these values off the stack and restoring the original state. Computer scientists often describe this type of behavior using a model known as a *state diagram*. Most state diagrams help illustrate state changes in the execution or operation of a computer system. Typically, circles are used to describe a state, and arrows are used to describe transitions between states.

Interrupt processing can be described using a state diagram in which normal processing is viewed as one type of state, and two types of transitions are allowed: maskable and non-maskable interrupts, each eventually leading to an interrupt processing state, which then eventually transitions to normal processing via a return transition.

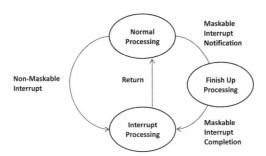

The state diagram is useful, because it helps to provide a visual representation of the difference between maskable and non-maskable interrupts. The maskable ones allow an intermediate state because the interrupt is less urgent, whereas the non-maskable ones require immediate interrupt handling.

Example: Use a state diagram to depict what might happen if some non-maskable interrupt were to occur during the processing of an unrelated maskable interrupt.

Answer: Let's assume that a maskable interrupt has occurred, and that the computer system is in the *Finish Up Processing* state. The resulting execution flow is shown in the state diagram below (follow the numbers to follow the flow):

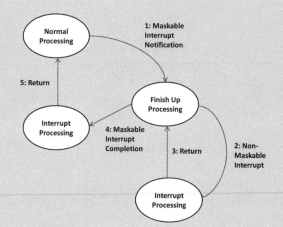

Note that it is possible for the system described by this state diagram to never return to normal processing if interrupts continue to occur forever.

As suggested above, if you take a moment to examine the flow in the example, you can easily imagine scenarios where one non-maskable interrupt after another continues to occur, resulting in some sort of infinite nesting of interrupt processing. It is precisely this type of unwanted condition that causes all sorts of problems in typical computers.

Unlike many other types of engineered systems, computer systems with behavior such as described above for interrupts, are susceptible to these types of so-called *run-time execution errors*. Identifying these problems before they occur is one of the central challenges in modern computer science.

16: Program Translation

You cannot trust code that you did not totally create yourself.

Ken Thompson

inary instructions, like 0110 1011, are referred to collectively as *machine language*. While machine language instructions are easily decoded by a CPU, they are not easy for humans to understand. As a result, programmers use a set of more human-readable instructions, such as LDA, JMP, and NOP, to write programs. These instructions are referred to as *assembly language*, and a program called an *assembler* translates assembly language instructions, one at a time, into the corresponding machine language instructions as follows:

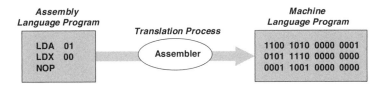

Now, if you are at all familiar with computers, then at some point in your life, you might have seen the code associated with an actual computer program. In all likelihood, this program did not look at all like assembly language or machine language. Instead, it was probably written in a language such as Java, Python, C++, or Visual Basic. Programs in these languages look sort of like the following:

```
print ("Hello, world.")
if x > 0 then y = 0 else y = 1
sum = (num1 + num2 + num3)
```

Programs in this form are said to be written in a *high-level programming language*. The major advantage of a high-level programming language is that humans can more easily understand what is going on, which makes it much easier to write more complex programs. The way high-level programming languages are translated into assembly language is via a program called a *compiler*. The translation process from high-level language, to assembly language, and ultimately to machine language is as follows:

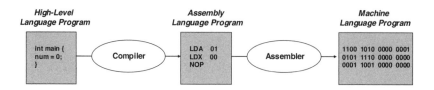

Example: A popular programming language that many young programmers enjoy using is called Python. If you want to write and execute a Python program on a personal computer, what translation tools would you need?

Answer: Python, it turns out, can be translated with a program, similar to a compiler, called an *interpreter*. In order to write, translate, and execute a Python program on your laptop, you would need to find an interpreter that will recognize and translate your Python code using commands provided by the operating system (e.g. Windows). This interpreter would have to also have the capability to then translate your code into the native assembly language code of the processor in your laptop (e.g., an Intel processor). If these two conditions are met, then you can write, translate, and execute Python programs on your computer.

One of the most popular programming languages today is called *Java*. It was created in 1995 by James Gosling who invented Java as part of his work on video set-top-boxes at Sun Microsystems. Programmers immediately liked the Java language and have used it to create many sorts of useful programs that we all use every day. Here is an example Java program that prints the phrase "Hello, world!"

```
public class Hello {
    public static void main (String[] args) {
        System.out.println("Hello, world!");
    }
}
```

Don't worry about trying to understand all the words and phrases in the program. It's just here to give you an idea of what Java programs look like. Another popular programming language called C++ was invented at AT&T by Bjarne Stroustroup. Here is the C++ version of the "Hello, world!" program:

```
#include <iostream>
int main()
{
    std::cout << "Hello, world!\n";
}
```

The programming language Python, mentioned above, includes most of the constructs that modern, powerful languages offer, but it also allows for the creation of simple programs that can be easily analyzed. Here is how a Python programmer would write the "Hello, World!" program:

```
print 'Hello, world!'
```

There are hundreds of different programming languages in use today, each with their respective strengths and weaknesses. In the end, most programmers select a language based on personal preference. What most computer scientists use, however, to teach programming concepts, is something called *pseudo-code*. This is a shorthand way to represent programs in a format that pretty much anyone can understand. Below is how we would write the "Hello, world!" program in pseudo-code:

```
begin
    print ("Hello, world!)
end
```

Pseudo code is useful because it avoids many of the little details required in a real programming language. It allows programmers to create and analyze software logic without having to worry about the details of the programming language, much of which might exist for reasons other than the primary purpose of the program. For example, many programs are written to include code that handles all sorts of errors that could occur during program execution. In addition, many programs include code that is written to provide assistance to the compilers and other program translation tools being used.

Pseudo-code focuses, instead, on just the basics needed to write a program. Computer scientists refer to this technique of separating out unnecessary details as *abstraction*. Many programmers believe that the ability to abstract detail is one of the most powerful abilities programmers can learn.

17: Constants, Variables, Types

One man's constant is another man's variable.

Alan Perlis

In order to understand how high-level programs are designed, it helps to look at some of the basic building blocks used by programmers in writing code. Most high-level programs begin with a section in which the program's *constants* and *variables* are *declared*. A constant is a symbol that will be associated with some value that will not change throughout the execution of the program. It is declared to help human beings read and understand the program. Here are a couple of example constant declarations:

```
constants
    pi = 3.141
    e = 2.718
```

These program statements assign the designated values to the specified constants. Once a constant is declared, the program can reference either the constant symbol or the numeric value, because they are synonymous. Constants are a key building block in designing readable programs.

A variable is a symbol that will be associated with some value that can change during the execution of the program. In order to control the values that can be associated with a given variable, programmers must do two things:

- *Initialization*: They must define the initial value for the variable when the program begins execution.

- *Variable Type*: They must define the *type* of values that are allowed to be associated with the variable during program execution. Virtually all programming languages include a set of predefined types such as Integer that can be used by programmers.

Below are example statements that assign an initial value and a predefined type to three variables:

```
variables
   integer age = 0
   real weight = 0.5
   string name = "Matt"
```

These declarations introduce three variables: age, weight, and name. The predefined types that are associated with these variables, respectively, are integer, real (numbers expressed as decimals), and string (sequences of characters). Their initial values are 0, 0.5, and "Matt", respectively. When the compiler translates the program, it will check that the initial values are of the correct type.

If a program assigns a type such as string to a variable in the declaration portion of a program, then the program cannot later assign some other data type to that variable. For example, if the declaration portion of a program defines some variable x to be of type string, then the program cannot include assignment of a numeric or other non-string value to that variable. If that were attempted in the code, the compiler would provide an error message during program translation.

Most programming languages also allow programmers to create *user-defined types*. For example, you might define a type that includes several colors; or you might define a type that includes some set of numbers; or whatever. Below are example type definitions:

```
types
    colors = {red, orange, yellow, blue}
    lucky_numbers = {23, 55, 87, 113}
```

As you would expect, variables can be declared to have a user-defined type as follows:

```
variables
    colors shirt = red
    lucky_numbers my_number = 55
```

Note in the above examples, that we chose names that were somewhat descriptive of the information associated with the name. Thus, rather than defining a variable of type color as X or Y, we used *shirt* because it is suggestive of the concept being modeled in the program.

Example: Create a user-defined type that would correspond to the planets in our solar system.

Answer: A user-defined type Planets could be defined as follows:

```
types
   planets = {Mercury, Venus, Earth, Mars,
              Jupiter, Saturn, Uranus, Neptune}
```

You might notice that the constant, variable, and type names we've used are single words. In fact, we even used the underscore '_' symbol to connect words to ensure that they were one word. You'll find that programming languages generally require this approach, because it helps the compiler. For example, suppose we defined a variable as follows:

```
variables
    lucky numbers my number = 55
```

Do you see how the compiler would have trouble knowing which words were being used to define the type, and which words were being used to define the variable? The type could be *lucky* and the variable declaration *numbers my number*; or the type could be *lucky numbers my* and the variable *number*; and so on. So most programming languages require that variables and constants be single words.

It is also essential that programmers use spaces in their programs properly. If you are writing a program and you run two words together that were intended to be separated by spaces, then you will confuse the compiler. For example, if you intend to declare some variable my_wallet, with a user-defined type wallet_types, as follows:

```
variables
    wallet_types my_wallet = 25.50
```

To reinfornce the importance of being careful when you program, suppose that you are sloppy with your coding and you forget to put a space between wallet_types and my_wallet, then the declaration would take on a completely different purpose as follows:

```
variables
    wallet_typesmy_wallet = 25.50
```

Also as suggested above, by selecting useful names, we help explain to readers of our program what the constants, variables, and types are used for. Words that are suggestive of their meaning and easy to remember are referred to by computer scientists as being *mnemonic* (pronounced *new-mon-ick*). This is important if the program you are writing will be used or maintained by some other programmer at a later time, which is common in most software companies.

Note finally that variables are assigned values in these program declarations using the "=" sign as an assignment operator. So, when we say that shirt = red, we're assigning that value to the variable. Some programming language designers preferred to use the operator := for assigning values to variables. We will generally use = throughout our examples in this book to denote assignment and == to denote equality.

18: Arrays

Doing linear scans over an associative array is like clubbing someone to death with a loaded Uzi.

Larry Wall

Programmers use data structures known as *arrays* to help manipulate data. They make the design of programs much easier by providing a convenient listing mechanism for many types of program operations. An array is a finite sequence of slots into which data can be held. Some beginning programmers like to think of them as long, horizontal cubby holes where data can be stored.

The front section or *declarative* portion of a program is where arrays are defined, usually as either constants or variables. Here is an example pseudo-code declaration:

integer digits [1 to 10]

This example introduces an array variable named digits which will have ten slots that are allowed to contain data of type integer. The compiler will allocate enough memory to hold the array. Each of the elements of the array is referred to by a numeric *index* as follows:

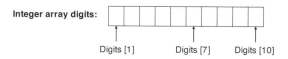

Suppose, for example, that a program assigns values to this array using indices as follows:

```
digits [1] = 4
digits [2] = 6
digits [3] = 2
```

The result is that the contents of the array, after the assignment, will look this way:

Integer array digits: | 4 | 6 | 2 | | | | | | |

By convention, programmers often depict arrays visually from left to right in a diagram, but there is nothing particularly special about that designation. Regardless of the method you prefer, you should try to maintain consistency.

Example: Create a user-defined type that would correspond to the planets in our solar system.

Answer: A user-defined type planets could be defined as follows:

```
types
    planets = {Mercury, Venus, Earth, Mars,
               Jupiter, Saturn, Uranus, Neptune}
```

Arrays are primarily useful because they allow programmers to maintain and manage lists. For example, you could write a program that tallies all the grades in a class using an array that has length equal to the number of students. Each slot in the array would then be used to store a student grade. Or you could create a program that uses an array to manage a list of numbers that you plan to manipulate in some way, such as sorting the list into order.

To illustrate arrays in use in a program, let's create a simple example that prints the values in an array of length 5. We'll assume that the statement *print ("Hello, world!")* in our program will result in the text "Hello, world!" being sent to the output device, which may be something like a monitor. Note that in most programming languages, the print command does not generally mean sending the output to a printer. This sometimes confuses new programmers.

Also, you'll see the use of \n in the program below. This simply tells the compiler to include a *carriage return* in the output. Carriage returns create a new line. In any event, here is our example:

```
program print_array
    integer list [0 to 4] = {0, 1, 2, 3, 4}
begin
    print (list[0]\n)
    print (list[1]\n)
    print (list[2]\n)
    print (list[3]\n)
    print (list[4]\n)
end
```

When this program executes, it will result in the following being displayed on the computer screen:

```
0
1
2
3
4
```

By the way, if we hadn't included the carriage returns in each of the print statements in our program, then the execution of the program would have produced the following:

```
01234
```

This is a simple enough example program, but it illustrates the basic use of an array variable. Most computer scientists agree that arrays, or at least some comparable list structure, play a central role in the implementation of virtually every useful computer program ever written. A similar structure, however, known as a *linked list*, can also be used to represent structured, ordered data. To illustrate the use of a linked list, let's examine a conceptual structure, similar to a stack, known as a *queue*.

In contrast to the LIFO functionality of a stack, a queue has a *first-in, first-out* (FIFO) type function. That is, just like people lining up in a queue to get into a movie theater, the first ones to arrive onto the queue are followed by others who arrive afterward – and are placed in order behind the first element. The queue is emptied by removing the first one to arrive, followed by others in the order in which they arrived. We refer to the placement of items into a FIFO queue as an *enqueue* operation and removal as a *dequeue* operation.

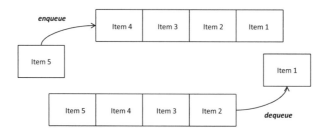

While queues can be implemented using arrays, linked lists can also be used. The way a linked list works is that elements of the structure – in this case, the queue – are associated with two specific components: the stored data and a so-called *reference*, also known as a *pointer,* to the next element in the queue. This allows for a chaining together of linked list nodes with the last node in the list linked to some terminator node that grounds the overall list.

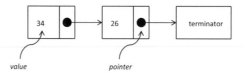

Many programming languages, especially those derived from the C programming language, include specific constructs for creating linked lists using pointers. Most programmers prefer using pointers to arrays because they provide for efficient traversal of their corresponding data structures, but new programmers sometimes find pointers and their associated arithmetic to be somewhat challenging.

19: Conditionals and Loops

As a rule, software systems do not work well until they have been used, and have failed repeatedly, in real applications.

David Parnas

You'll recall from above that we used *jump* and *branch* logic to control execution flow in assembly language programs. Both statements caused program execution to simply hop from one statement in a program to another. For high level language programming, however, we will require much more powerful flow control constructs that allow for the creation of *conditionals* and *loops*.

The most basic conditional statement in programming is known as *if-then-else*. This statement is designed to test some condition, and then execute accordingly. Almost every piece of software you will ever see will include some form of if-then-else conditional statement. Here is a simple example:

```
if country == America then
    print ("Hello"\n)
else
    print ("Ciao"\n)
fi
```

Notice the technique common in computer science to terminate the *if* portion of the statement with the reverse *fi*. This symmetric approach helps programmers create if-then-else statements that are clearer to read and easier to understand. The conditional portion of an if-then-else statement where a logical expression is used to determine the appropriate branching in the statement can also be somewhat more involved as shown below:

```
if country == America and mood == happy then
    print ("Hello"\n)
else
    print ("Ciao"\n)
fi
```

In addition, the if-then-else statement can be connected into a structured combination of arbitrary complexity. Sometimes, this can become more complicated than it should, but generally, programmers find it useful to be able to string together their conditional logic into different forms. Below is a simple example:

```
if country == America then
    print ("Hello"\n)
else if country == Italy then
        print ("Ciao"\n)
    else
        print ("Bonjour"\n)
    fi
fi
```

Now that we've looked at the if-then-else conditional, let's look at a related construct known as a *loop*. The most basic of all loop constructs is the *for-loop*. This works by counting out some number of rounds in the loop by using a special index variable. Here's an example:

```
for index = 1 to 10 do
    print (list [index])
od
```

What happens in this simple example loop is that the index variable starts with value 1, which implies that the first element of the index array will be printed. Then the index variable is incremented to 2, and the second element of the index variable will be printed. This will continue until the tenth element of the index variable is printed and then the loop terminates.

Note that if we had started the index value at 0 and successively incremented to 9, then the overall functionality would have been the same. Selection of the optimal index starting value is really up to the programmer; most programming experts agree, however, that the most important consideration is to be consistent. Throughout the examples in this book, we generally start index values with 1.

Example: Use a *for-loop* to write a small snippet of code to zero out an integer array A with length ten.

Answer: The code snippet is as follows:

```
for index = 1 to 10 do
    A[index] = 0
od
```

A common way to use for-loops is to examine strings. If you recall, strings are groups of individual characters that make up meaningful words and phrases to humans, but not to computers. Using for-loops to examine each individual character of a string can give the string meaning to the computer.

For example, a website that requires certain criteria for passwords, (at least one letter, symbol, number, etc.) may utilize for-loops to do this. Similar to our previous examples of for-loops, this code would execute commands as many times as a certain index tells it to. In the above code, this index is an array with length 10, but in a password analyzing for-loop the index would be the actual password, or string.

Another loop construct is called a *while-loop*. This works in a similar manner, but rather than counting out an index in advance, the while-loop tests some condition at the end of the loop to determine whether to continue on, or repeat another round of the loop. Here's an example:

```
index = 1
while index < 11 do
    print (list [index])
    index++
od
```

What happens in this loop is that we begin by explicitly creating and initializing an index value to 1. Loops are often dependent on such an index. The loop then begins by testing to see if the value of the index is less than 11. As long as this is true, the list element is printed and then the index is incremented. The notation *index++* means that the present value of the index should be increased by 1. You can see that the loop will quit when the value of the index is incremented beyond 10.

A variation on the while loop is the *repeat-until loop*, which continues a loop over and over until some designated condition is met after execution of one iteration. Here is the code for the list printing program shown above, but this time with the repeat-until construct:

```
index = 1
repeat
    print (list [index])
    index++
until index == 11
```

Programmers generally try to assign the most natural loop construct to the code being written. In any of the cases, however, it helps for programmers to consider the conditions that are true before and after the execution of a loop (or any other code, for that matter). As we alluded to earlier in the book, computer scientists usually refer to the conditions that are true before some code executes as the *preconditions*, and to the conditions that are true after that code executes as the *postconditions*. If you study computer science, you are likely to run into these concepts as you learn to logically analyze program execution.

Spotlight: Edsger W. Dijkstra

From the early 1960's until his death in 2002, Professor Edsger W. Dijkstra had a profound influence on the development of computer science. Born in 1930 in the Netherlands, Edsger began his studies in physics, but quickly moved toward the study of computers and software. He would eventually become a professor at Eindhoven University of Technology and then later at the University of Texas at Austin.

Some consider Dijkstra's most famous accomplishments to be his algorithm for computing the *shortest path* between two points in a graph. To this day, network systems on the Internet make use of Dijkstra's approach. Dijkstra also pioneered many of the concepts used in operating systems including the use of *semaphores*. In his later years, Dijkstra focused much of his research on using mathematics to improve the quality of software.

One of Dijkstra's more interesting accomplishments was the publication of his so-called *EWD series*. Each note in the EWD series was handwritten and eventually copied or faxed by computer scientists around the world. Dijkstra covered all sorts of topics in his EWD series, from highly mathematical works, to sometimes biting and often sarcastic criticisms of individual computer scientists and corporations. For his EWD series, many people credit Dijkstra with being the original *blogger*.

20: Algorithms

Controlling complexity is the essence of computer programming.

Brian Kernighan

An *algorithm* is a sequence of steps that describes precisely how some task should be carried out. Purists like to say that algorithms are procedures that work as planned every time. They often use the term *heuristics* for procedures that may produce uncertain or unpredictable results. We will not spend much time here on the subtle distinctions between algorithms and heuristics – rather, we will simple assume that an algorithm defines some step-by-step procedure.

In everyday life, cooking recipes and driving instructions are good examples of algorithms. They lay out a basic sequence of steps that result in a well-defined purpose being met. In computer science, programs follow specific algorithms that the programmer either invents or reuses. Most of the best algorithms are ones that have been designed by smart people, and then submitted to open scrutiny by reviewers and users.

In the software community, a distinction arises between so-called *open-source* software, where the algorithm and associated implementation are open to review, investigation, and reuse. In comparison, so-called *proprietary* software is owned and controlled by some group that prefers to keep the algorithm and associated code secret.

In order to understand how algorithms are used, let's begin with a familiar example of an everyday algorithm that is used outside the context of computing:

```
begin Morning Algorithm
    alarm, wake, rise, brush, shower
    if disheveled then comb else don't
    dress, eat, school
end Morning Algorithm
```

You can see that this algorithm is a sequence of steps that describes how your morning should go. It gives you a pretty reasonable idea of what is intended to be accomplished, but it also abstracts details that are not important to the algorithm (such as where your comb is, or what specific type of food you eat, etc.). If one follows the algorithm, it should work the same each time.

Computer scientists sometimes use a diagram called a *flowchart* to design and describe an algorithm. Here is the flowchart for the Morning Algorithm:

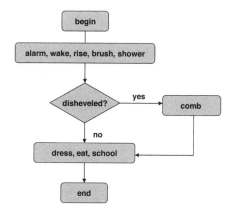

A structure such as a flowchart is intended to help human beings better understand how the algorithm works. Its visual representation sometimes can be easier to follow than programming language descriptions. When additional diagrams and words are used to help humans in this way, computer scientists refer to this as the *documentation* of the program. Without proper documentation, complex algorithms can be next to impossible for human beings to understand.

It should be obvious that all sorts of errors can arise in even the most trivial algorithms. As programs grow in size and complexity, the likelihood of errors cropping in grows accordingly. Documentation, such as a flow chart, therefore becomes especially important when an algorithm contains some problem that must be diagnosed and removed. Documentation also helps programmers analyze the feasibility of an algorithm, including whether it accomplishes its objective.

Another important issue is how quickly an algorithm is designed to execute. Some algorithms are designed to run in an *efficient* manner. Others are designed to run more inefficiently. To illustrate this concept, let's spend some time looking at an algorithm for searching an unsorted list called *linear search*. What this algorithm does, essentially, is check each element of a list for the desired element, continuing on until the value is found or not. The basic structure of the algorithm can be depicted as shown in the flowchart below.

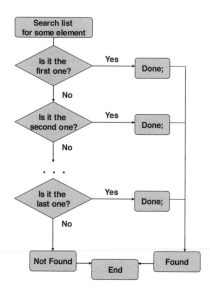

One of the more difficult aspects of programming involves translating an algorithmic description, such as the flow chart above, into code. Many different techniques have been proposed for doing this, but in the end, each programmer needs to develop their own mental tools for developing correct code from an algorithmic description. Some programmers like to use mathematical descriptions, others like to draw pictorial diagrams, and others use even more personal approaches.

An important area of research in computer science includes specifying an algorithm more formally than as a flow chart. The algorithm would instead be specified using mathematics and the code would be essentially derived from the specification. Such formal specification is a promising technique for future programmers but remains an elusive goal in current programming practice.

The search program written in pseudo-code that finds an integer in an unsorted array of integers of length n can be written as shown in the example below:

```
program search
-- assume A is an unsorted integer array
-- assume program searches for integer x
-- assume found is an initially false variable
begin
    index = 1
    repeat
        if A[index] == x then found
        else
            index = index + 1
        fi
    until found or index > length(A)
end
```

As we have said, this linear search technique is efficient for a very small list, but might not be exactly the best approach if the list is very long. Computer scientists spend a great deal of time trying to make algorithms run more quickly. This process, known as *optimization*, is important because it results in a better and faster experience for users of computer systems.

Computer scientists have developed a technique known as *Big O* notation that allows for the comparison of run-time efficiencies for different algorithms. If an algorithm is performing a linear task such as the search program shown above, then the size of the input or number of items being processed is used as the basis for measuring the linear complexity of the algorithm. The notation used for an algorithm operating on n input items would be shown as $O(n)$.

Computer scientists generally try to improve the efficiency of their algorithms by introducing clever heuristic approaches that reduce the amount of time required to accomplish a task. As you progress in your study of computer science, you will be introduced to algorithms that change the runtime characteristics from linear to logarithmic, quadratic, factorial, and many other interesting mathematical characterizations of run-time complexity.

21: Sorting and Searching

Any inaccuracies in this index may be explained by the fact that it has been sorted with the help of a computer.

Donald Knuth

You'll recall from above that we outlined a simple strategy for performing a straight linear search from a list of unsorted numbers. The algorithm started at the top and checked for the searched-for element one number at a time down the list. For very long lists, this linear process can take a long time and is thus considered inefficient for many types of practical applications.

One problem that arises in straight linear searching of an unsorted list of numbers is that execution of the algorithm must continue to the end of the list if the searched-for element is not found sooner. In a sorted list, the execution can terminate once the list has been examined past the point where the desired item would have been located. On average, this can reduce average execution time by half.

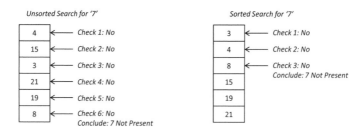

To improve on search efficiency, we will therefore need to first introduce an algorithm that sorts a list. Many different algorithms exist for sorting a list, but one approach that has been popular with computer scientists is known as *bubble sort*. The basic idea in bubble sort is that during successive rounds of interim sorting of a list, values "bubble" up to the top. Below is the pseudo-code for a bubble_sort procedure on an array of integers:

```
-- Bubble Sort on an array A of integers
-- No declarative section for convenience

    program bubble_sort
    begin
      repeat
        swapped = false
          for index = 1 to length(A) - 1 do
            if A[index - 1] > A[index] then
              swap(A[index - 1], A[index])
              swapped = true
            fi
          od
      until not swapped
    end
```

The way bubble_sort works is that the array is traversed from top to bottom, swapping successive values if they are not in order. This process continues until the list is traversed from top to bottom, and all items are in order. The variable *swapped* is used to remember if any value was swapped during a traversal (designated by the *for* loop).

One way to better understand algorithms involves the use of a *graphical visualization*. The Internet is filled with example visualizations of how sorting and searching algorithms work. Below is one example found on the Internet for bubble sort that depicts each line as an element of a list. You can see from the graph how each element bubbles up to its appropriate spot in the final sorted list.

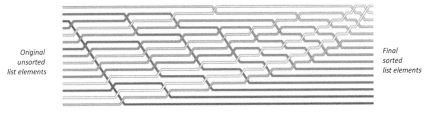

Original
unsorted
list elements

Final
sorted
list elements

Flow of the algorithm showing successive swaps

Computer scientists have devised many other algorithms for sorting lists, includes ones for placing items in both numerical and lexicographical order. Some popular algorithms include the following:

- *Merge Sort*: This algorithm is excellent for operational environments that allow multiple, parallel processors to execute the code. The Internet has many descriptions and example implementations of this sorting solution.
- *Shell Sort*: This algorithm is efficient in terms of code size and memory usage during runtime. If you must perform sorting on an old, inefficient computer with few resources, this might be your choice. You can learn more on the Internet about Shell Sort as well.

Now that we know how to sort a list, we can introduce an improved and more *efficient* search algorithm called *binary search* that will find a desired element in a sorted list more quickly than a linear search. The only requirement for binary search is that the list first be sorted (regardless of the sorting algorithm used). Here is the pseudo-code:

```
-- Binary Search of a sorted array A of integers
-- No declarative section included for convenience

    program binary_search
    begin
      n = length (A)
      low = 0
      high = n - 1
      while (low <= high) do
        mid = (low + high) / 2
        if (A[mid] > value) then
          high = mid - 1
        else if (A[mid] < value) then
              low = mid + 1
            else
              print (mid, " found"\n)
            fi
        fi
      od
      print ("not found"\n)
    end
```

The general strategy for Binary Search is as follows: The search starts with the middle number in the list. If that number is right, then the process is done; but if the middle number is greater than the searched-for number, then the search moves to the lower half of the list. If the middle number is less than the searched-for number, then the search moves to the top half of the list. Now let's step through how the actual algorithm implements this idea.

The program sets variables low and high to be the lower and upper bounds on the list being searched. Note that it does this by setting the lower bound to be 0 and the upper bound to be one less than the size of the array. So if the array is size 9, then the lower bound is 0 and the upper bound is 8.

The while loop then continually checks the middle value to see if it's greater than or less than the value being searched. Depending on the result, the lower and upper bounds are changed and the loop repeats.

Here is an execution trace for the program, assuming a list of five sorted integers being searched for the value 5:

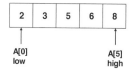

The while loop checks to see if low (which is 0) is less than high (which is 4). The middle index value will be 2, so the program checks to see if A[2] is greater than the value 5 (it is not), or less than the value 5 (it is not). So the program, in this case, prints that it found the value 5.

If the program had not found the desired number on this first try, then it would have returned to the loop and executed the same process on new upper and lower bounds. If the number being searched for was in the lower half of the array, then the new upper bound would be the middle. If, on the other hand, the number being searched for was in the upper half of the array, then the new lower bound would be the middle.

It would be a good idea for you to practice some execution traces for different searched-for values and different sorted lists. Most computer scientists learned the art of searching from a famous pair of books called *Fundamental Algorithms* written by Donald Knuth from Stanford University. Just about every computer scientist in the world has those books on their shelves.

22: Subroutines

*All problems in computer science can be solved by another
level of indirection.*

Butler Lampson

T he programs we've written so far in this book begin at the start of
the program code, execute based on the program logic, and then
terminate at the end. If you were tracing the execution flow with
your finger, you'd be mostly starting at the top of the page and then
moving downward (ignoring the fact that loops sometimes bounce you
back up temporarily).

A powerful programming tool called *subroutines*, however, is used
commonly by computer scientists to promote a more dramatic effect on
program execution. Subroutines allow for the creation of new programmer-
defined abstract components that can be used in a computer program. For
example, let's suppose that you start with a program that looks roughly like
the following:

```
program test_with_no_subroutines
begin
  command_1
  command_2
  command_3
end
```

Each of the three commands in this test program is presumably
defined by the language designer and understood by the compiler. For
example, the first command might accept some user input from a keyboard,
the second might perform some sort of computation, and the third might
print some output on the screen. These would be done with standard
commands in the programming language being used. In many cases, the

language reserves so-called *keywords* for these well-defined and understood functions.

But what if the programmer wanted to create new commands? Perhaps these commands might be custom-designed to perform tasks that would be useful for the program being written. In some sense, this could be thought of as extending the power of the programming language being used to include new functions, also often referred to as methods, that the programmer wants to incorporate into programs. This extension would be done using subroutines. The concept is illustrated below:

```
program test_with_subroutines
begin
  procedure_1
  procedure_2
  command_3
end

subroutine procedure_1
begin
  command_1
end

subroutine procedure_2
begin
  command_2
end
```

This test_with_subroutines program has two subroutines and will perform exactly the same function as the test_with_no_subroutines example. The execution flow is shown in the diagram below:

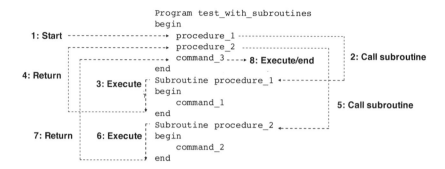

If you trace the program flow following the numbered comments in the figure above, you can see how the processing starts in the top program and then goes back and forth between the subroutines until it finally terminates. Another effective way to depict aspects of program flow with subroutines involves the use of a state diagram:

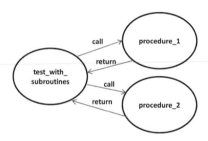

One problem with any state diagram is that it will not capture the flow of the program effectively. State diagrams are excellent at describing possible execution traces and flows, but not always great at describing the actual flows that are followed during execution of a real computer program. Programmers therefore have to be very careful how they use these types of tools.

Subroutines allow programmers to create abstract *objects* that perform specified tasks and that can be called in a main program. This is a powerful technique and is used extensively in computer science. In fact, when lots of different subroutines are collected together for use in a program, this collection is referred to as a *program library*. Some companies exist to simply write useful program libraries for programmers.

When subroutines are designed to return values, they are often called *functions*. Many languages such as Python use this concept to allow for more powerful creation of useful objects without having to create separate variables for passing information between main programs and their subroutines. An important concept in the implementation of a function, however, is the so-called *return* of a value. For example, if a function is called to add two numbers, then it must return the answer. Our next chapter will demonstrate how this is done using a construct known as an *argument*.

When related functions are provided together as a group for programmers to use, the result is often referred to as an *application programming interface* or *API*. An API can be viewed as a menu of services available to programmers, and these services are implemented, essentially, as programmed subroutines. The general terminology is that the program invoking or *calling* API functions is referred to as a *calling program*.

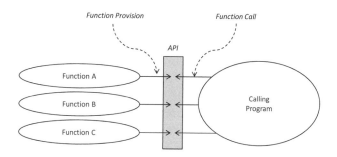

A final point about subroutines is that some programmers refer to subroutines or API functions as *software tools*. This allows for the reuse of code in many different contexts, with saves time and allows programmers to build on the work of others. Thus, programmers often download free (or even purchase) software tools that help them write more effective programs.

23: Arguments

Numerical subroutines should deliver results that satisfy simple, useful mathematical laws whenever possible.

Donald Knuth

This chapter is not about fighting with your friends. Rather it's about special mechanisms called *arguments* that are used in most programming languages to make subroutines more useful and powerful in programs. As suggested in the previous chapter, arguments are special parameters that are embedded in subroutines so that they can act as functions, accepting and returning values with calling programs.

Let's illustrate with an example. Suppose that you wish to write a program in some programming language that adds two numbers together and that you wish to do it using a subroutine called *add*. It should be obvious that when the calling program invokes the subroutine *add*, it should do so with the two numbers to be added. That is, the calling program should provide these two arguments to the subroutine as inputs, and the corresponding subroutine would then provide a return value based on its computation.

The diagram below shows this for a calling program that wishes to add 5 and 6. This is done by providing these two values as arguments to a subroutine that then performs the addition, and provides back the result of the addition as a return value.

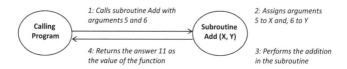

The concept of a return value for subroutines is useful in programming because it allows the programmer to use a subroutine call based on the type of value it returns. For example, the addition subroutine implied in the diagram above returns an integer, so the programmer can write small program snippets such as the following (assuming the subroutine is called *add* and takes two arguments).

```
add (5, 6) + add (7, 8) + add (2, 3)
```

Let's look at a typical pseudo-code representation of a subroutine for addition that actually does take two numeric arguments, and that returns the result as a functional value. Note that for simplicity in these and later examples, we will not include the declarative portions of the programs where the variables and associated types are defined. In a real program that is designed for translation by a compiler, these declarative sections are important and cannot be removed.

In the example below, we also hard code the two values 5 and 6 to be added together for simplicity. In any realistic addition program, the user would be prompted to provide input that would provide two (or more) values to be added. Hard coding the values as shown below renders the program useless for every application except the unusual case of adding these two specific numbers.

```
program addition_example
begin
  x = 5
  y = 6
  sum = add (x, y)
end

subroutine add (i, j)
begin
  return (i + j)
end
```

This example program shows the subroutine add being called with the two hard-coded numbers 5 and 6 that are referred to as *arguments* to the subroutine. You can see that they are values passed from the main function and then lined up with the arguments i and j in the subroutine. The subroutine also has a statement called *return* that sends the final summation value calculated by the subroutine back to the main program. This concept of a subroutine function accepting input, processing based on the input, and then providing back output is central to modern programming.

Example: Write a subtraction program with a corresponding subroutine that subtracts two hard coded numbers (use 10 and 5).

Answer: The code can be written as follows to subtract 5 from 10:

```
program subtraction_example
begin
    x = 10
    y = 5
    result = subtract (x, y)
end

subroutine subtract (i, j)
begin
    return (i - j)
end
```

One feature often found in a typical programming language involves declaring the type of return value provided by a subroutine. This would look like the following:

```
integer subroutine subtract (i, j)
```

When this is done, the subroutine is often referred to specifically as an integer function. To even more carefully further specify the function, the types associated with the two input arguments are also often declared in the subroutine specification as follows:

```
integer subroutine subtract (integer i, j)
```

You can see how this type of careful specification helps programmers avoid errors, and certainly makes the program easier to understand – but only after you understand the syntax and the rules associated with the programming language.

Returning to our addition subroutine example, is sometimes tricky for students to understand how the call to the subroutine uses variables x and y, whereas the actual subroutine uses variables i and j. The answer lies in the fact that subroutines are intended to be useful for many different programs. Thus, if another subroutine, for example, wants to call the add subroutine, then it can do so with whatever variables or values it wants to add. One way to visualize this in the code above is to connect the variables as follows:

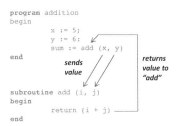

Let's introduce two more functions called *input* and *print* that both use arguments. The input function accepts user generated data, usually from a keyboard. The print function sends data to an output device, usually a screen. Both can be viewed either as commands in the programming language. Typical uses are shown below:

```
input (score1, score2)
print ("hello, world")
```

Let's now use these functions to write a slightly more interesting program that adds two numbers that a user types in, and then displays the output on a screen:

```
program addition
begin
    print ("Please type in two integers:   ")
    input (value1, value2)
    sum = add (value1, value 2)
    print (sum)
end

subroutine add (i, j)
begin
    return (i + j)
end
```

This program is clearly more interesting than the first *add* program because it allows the user to input a pair of integers and to see the result printed on the screen. If we wanted to continually allow the user to keep entering pairs of integers to be added, we can wrap the program in a *do-loop*. We need to create an exit condition, so we'll tell the user to type in two 0's to quit. Here's the associated program:

```
program addition
begin
  print ("This adds integers you type in.")
  print ("Type in two 0's when you are done.")
  do
    print ("Please type in two integers:  ")
    input (value1, value2)
    sum = add (value1, value 2)
    print (sum)
  until value1 = value2 = 0
end

subroutine add (i, j)
begin
  return (i + j)
end
```

To continue adding new features to program such as the one above, most programmers follow a process known as *iterative design*, where successive versions of code are created, each with some new desired feature. This approach has the advantage of allowing for small, incremental improvements in software, which makes it easier to find errors that might creep into the coding process.

24: Recursion

In order to understand recursion, one must first understand recursion.

Anonymous

The topic of *recursion*, which is central to computer science, is fun to learn about, but requires a bit of thinking. Some people think of recursion as a sort of circular reasoning; for example, you sometimes see definitions of concepts that reference the concept being defined. Here is an example:

Definition: Recursion,
  See Recursion.

This whimsical definition of recursion is circular because you never make any progress. In fact, you find yourself in an infinite loop constantly trying to define recursion, only to find that the definition of recursion is recursion, and so on. If you programmed something like this using a subroutine that *calls itself*, here is what might happen:

```
subroutine recursive_call
begin
    print ("Hello, world!  ")
    recursive_call
end
```

The result of executing this program would be the following printed output:

Hello, world! Hello, world! Hello, world! Hello, world! (. . . and on and on)

111

Mathematics provides a hint as to how recursion can be made more useful by allowing it to actually terminate at some point. It does so with a form of logical reasoning known as *induction*. The way inductive reasoning works is that it first involves a *base concept* such as: "The number 1 is an integer." It then involves an *induction step* such as: "If some number is an integer, then the next higher number is also an integer." When you put the base concept and induction step together, you can draw logical conclusions.

For example, using the two example statements made above about integers, we can *prove* that 3 is an integer. Here's how:

Base Concept: The number 1 is an integer.
Induction Step: If the number 1 is an integer, then the number 2 is an integer.
Induction Step: If the number 2 is an integer, then the number 3 is an integer.

This form of reasoning is very close to how recursion works in a computer program. Let's look at an example subroutine, one that calculates the factorial value of a number n that is passed to the subroutine as an argument. The result is returned to the calling program. (By the way, you'll hopefully remember that "6 factorial," also written as 6!, is equal to 6 x 5 x 4 x 3 x 2 x 1):

```
subroutine factorial (n)
begin
    if n = 1 then
        return 1
    else
        return n x factorial (n-1)
    fi
end
```

This subroutine starts with the value of n being passed by the calling program; let's suppose for the sake of discussion that this number is 2. What will happen is that the first test is whether 2 is equal to 1 (which it is not). So the program will execute the "else" portion of the conditional. It will therefore return the value of n times the value of the factorial subroutine using n-1 as the new argument!

So the factorial subroutine will now execute with argument n = 1. This will cause the subroutine now to return the value 1 since the "if" portion of the conditional will evaluate true. This value is then passed to the original subroutine call and will be multiplied by n to compute the final return value of 2.

The diagram below illustrates the execution trace for this program in a more visual manner:

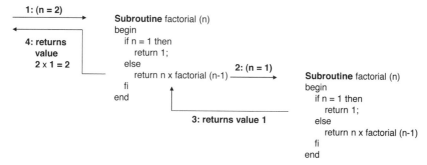

The diagram shows that for 2!, the subroutine is called twice: once for n = 2, and then again for n = 1. To compute 15!, the subroutine would be called 15 times. Computer scientists refer to each individual call of a subroutine as an *instantiation*. In addition, these subroutine instantiations can be referred to as *processes*, a topic that is important in the design of computer operating systems.

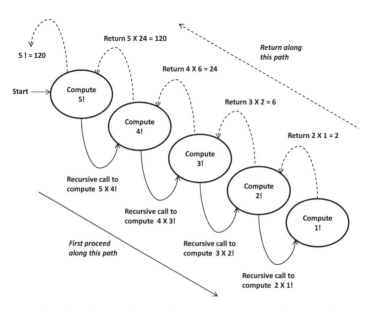

To visualize the flow of process execution between individual subroutine instantiations, the flow for calculating factorial – assuming n = 5 for the purpose of this illustration – can be depicted using the state shown above. The state diagram is viewed from the start arrow at the left of the chart, and then following the succession of recursive factorial calls from 5! down to 1!, as the initial processing flow. Once the program has reached 1!, it then begins its journey back up, returning a succession of answers to the next recursive process.

Example: Sketch a recursive function that computes the greatest common divisor (GCD) of two numbers.

Answer: The pseudo-code can be written as follows:

```
subroutine gcd (x, y)
begin
    if y = 0 then
       return y
    else
       return gcd (y, x mod y)
    fi
end
```

Understanding recursion in computer science is non-trivial, and represents one of the most subtle and challenging concepts we've examined thus far. Do not be discouraged if it takes you some time to understand how this important notion is used in program design. Eventually, you will understand – and it is worth the time and effort, because recursion provides a powerful tool for implementing effective algorithms.

25: Syntax and Grammar

There are two ways to write error-free programs; only the third one works.

Alan Perlis

Every program is written in a specific format that carefully defined by the *syntax* of the programming language being used. Syntax will differ from one language to another, but they all generally define programs as starting with some designation of the program name, and ending with some word or symbol that marks its end. The program is thus everything in between.

In spite of the differences between the syntax of programming languages, there are enough common approaches that we can generalize using pseudo-code to explain the basic and common concepts. Below, for example, is a high-level syntax outline for the programs we've been writing in pseudo-code:

```
program sample_program
   . . .
begin
   . . .
end
```

This outline suggests that a program begins with the word **program**. Then it lists the name of the program, followed by some other various declarative program elements, designated by the three dots. The program then lists the word **begin**, followed again by some other program statement elements (three dots again). The program then finishes with the word **end**.

A program called a compiler uses the syntactic rules of a language to perform translation to assembly language. Compilers look specifically for special words in the syntax called *keywords* that help define structure.

In the example above, the words **program**, **begin**, and **end** are all keywords and the compiler uses these to understand the various sections of the program.

If a programmer forgets to follow proper syntax in a program, then the compiler will not translate the program properly, perhaps issuing an error message. As you would imagine, the compiler program would begin by searching for these important keywords to determine where and how to process the program.

Computer scientists refer collectively to the formal rules for how programs are written as a *grammar*. The challenge is that computer scientists need to be a lot more specific about what is allowed in a program than just writing three dots, as we did above. They need to define the specific syntactic rules for programmers to follow, and need to give the compiler the specific rules it should use in translating a program.

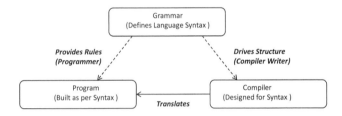

Four decades ago, two pioneering computer scientists named John Backus and Peter Naur invented a format for defining a program grammar. Their notation is called *Backus-Naur Form* or just *BNF* for short. The way BNF works is that it defines a program in terms of its specific components and subcomponents. Suppose, for example, that we wish to define the syntax for a program using the outline shown above. We would write the BNF as follows:

```
<program> =
    program <program name>
      <declarations>
    begin
      <main body>
    end
```

Anything written like <this> designates something that requires further definition, whereas anything written in **bold** will actually be included as is in the program. All keywords will be listed in bold. We know from this BNF that <program name>, <declarations>, and <main body> are the three portions of the program that need more definition. Let's look at an example of the declaration portion in BNF.

```
<declarations> =
    types
      <type definitions>
    constants
      <constant declarations>
    variables
      <variable declarations>
```

This grammar implies that every declaration portion always includes a types, constants, and variables section. Since we know that in most programming languages, each of these sections is optional, the BNF requires a means for designating such options. It does this using square braces in [this] manner. A section written like [this] is interpreted as optional. Here is an improved definition of the declarations portion of a program:

```
<declarations> =
    [types
      <type definitions>]
    [constants
      <constant declarations>]
    [variables
      <variable declarations>]
```

An interesting effect of this definition is that it allows the case where all three sections for types, constants, and variables are not present. This has been the case for the various example programs we're written in the previous discussions.

To define more specifically how the <main body> syntax is organized, we would begin with the recognition that every main body in a program is a succession of *statements* that perform some useful function in the program. For example, assigning a value to a variable, or performing some condition or loop calculation, or calling a subroutine, are all examples of statements. Thus we might define the main body of our programs as follows in BNF:

```
<main body > =
    {<statement>}*
```

The designation {<statement>}* is intended to mean zero or more instances of statement definitions. This implies that the main body of a program could be empty (zero statements), or it could be one statement, or it could be many statements. In any event, our BNF definition suggests that every main body is some sequence of statements that will allow us to write our program.

Example: Assuming the syntax for *sentences* is defined by <sentence>, create a simple grammar for *paragraphs*.

Answer: The grammar would be defined as a sequence of one or more sentences as follows:

```
<paragraph> =
    <sentence> {<sentence>}*
```

We could continue on, and any grammar designer would have to continue with the process until everything is defined, but readers should have the general idea of how grammars work from our examples above. Compiler writers, in particular, must peruse the grammar very carefully in order to write translation programs for a given language. In fact, the grammar provides a roadmap for exactly how the compiler will operate.

Programmers generally have a less tedious task, in that they generally only need to understand enough about the language syntax and associated semantics to write whatever program they have in mind. They generally do not need to understand 100% of the syntax any more than someone needs to understand 100% of the English language to speak.

Spotlight: Donald Knuth

Born in 1938, *Donald Knuth* completed his Ph.D. degree in mathematics from the California Institute of Technology in 1963. Knuth soon accepted a position as a professor at Stanford University, where he would remain for decades. In his early years, Knuth immersed himself in what he dubbed *"The Art of Computer Programming."* This passion for programming became the basis for three important volumes by this same name. These volumes are arguably the most famous books ever written on programming.

Generations of programmers have learned the design and implement algorithms from Professor Knuth. His works on sorting and searching lists are essential elements in any computer scientist's education. Knuth also made important contributions to the style of writing computer programs. He introduced, for example, a novel approach to the writing of a program, where the documentation and the code are actually readable in an interesting way by humans. He called the approach *literate programming.*

In 1974, Professor Knuth was the recipient of the prestigious *Turing Award*, granted by the Association for Computing Machinery (ACM). Computer scientists view this award as roughly equivalent to winning the Nobel Prize (unfortunately, there is no Nobel Prize for computer science).

26: Software Engineering

There are only two acceptable models of development: "think and analyze" or "years and years of testing in thousands of machines."

Linus Torvalds

Programming is generally viewed as an activity done by a single person; however, very large programs usually require that multiple people be involved. In fact, the gaming software that you probably play at home was most likely developed by a team of professional *software engineers*. These teams can become quite large. A computer-generated animated movie, for example, might require literally *hundreds* of software engineers, working on millions of lines of program code!

In order to build software that large, software engineers have to organize themselves and their work. They do this using something they call a *methodology*. For large software, the methodology is usually described as a series of different tasks that must be performed by software engineering groups. The most famous methodology is known as the *waterfall model* which is shown below:

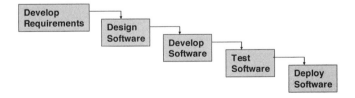

The model is called waterfall, because the sequence of activities looks sort of like steps with water running down the top. Almost every major software engineering project follows this model. But what has happened is that software engineers have noticed that as they work through the steps in the waterfall model, that they sometimes uncover mistakes.

121

During design, for example, they sometimes realize that they made a mistake in the requirements activity; or during testing, they realize that a mistake might have been made during design; and so on. This has led to a refinement of the waterfall model as follows:

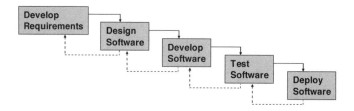

In this refined waterfall model, you can see that a series of backtracking steps are introduced into the methodology. This backtracking is referred to by software engineers as *interleaving*. The process of returning from one step in the process to a previous step is known as a *feedback loop*. Managers hate when projects get into an endless sequence of feedback loop steps, because it impedes progress toward the software engineering goal.

As a result, most professional software engineers will tell you how important it is to spend as much time in the earliest steps as possible to get things correct. In fact, when most software engineers discuss the amount of time that should be allocated to the various processes, they will show you two different graphs.

The first shown below with the solid line is the typical, non-optimal allocation of time in a software project, with the majority of time spent on developing software. The second allocation, however, also shown below using a dashed line, is more optimal and allocates the majority of time to the requirements and design phases.

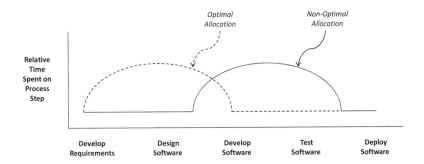

In practical software engineering settings, it has been generally agreed upon that the waterfall model provides a useful guide, but that in the rapidly changing world of technology, with increasing pressures from businesses to generate software more quickly, the model is considered too constraining. This is a controversial view, because software has so consistently been riddled with errors that many observers believe the extra constraints are necessary. Nevertheless, an iterative model, often referred to as the *spiral model*, has been more popular with software engineers.

In the spiral model, an initial version of code is created quickly by software designers. This early version is often referred to as *prototype* or *alpha* code. This release is created to provide an early view of how the software will work so that refinements can be made, often with inputs from a user base. This input is then fed into a development process that results in a new version often referred to as *beta* code.

As you would expect, a beta release is more mature than the alpha release, and provides a more effective means for obtaining additional feedback from users. A beta release is still, however, viewed as an early release that requires additional scrutiny and use before it will begin to approach a final, usable form.

This succession of iterative software releases and their associated analysis can be visually depicted as follows:

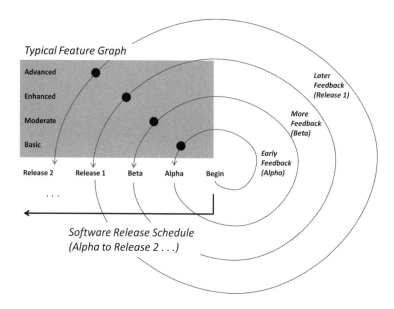

The spiral model is easy to follow, starting from the innermost point. Alpha code is developed and provided for feedback, this becoming the initial point on a release schedule, as well as the initial basic feature set. A succession of refinements is then performed, each advancing the release schedule, and increasing the features in the software being produced. In addition to the waterfall and spiral models, software engineers have developed recommendations on the best ways to develop large software. These include the following:

- *Structured Design*: Software engineers follow a structured design process in large software projects. This allows for common design components in all software developed. They all follow, for example, common documentation procedures, naming methods for programs and subroutines, common techniques for type, variable, and constant definitions, and so on. This way, you don't end up with dozens of different styles, approaches, and methods.

- *Modular Components*: Software engineers have determined that the best way to build large programs is by putting many, many smaller *modules* together. This basic principle of software modularity is one that a famous computer scientist named David Parnas was one of the chief proponents of. He wrote several famous papers that many software engineers read and incorporated into their large software projects.

- *Productivity Measurements*: Early software engineers were tempted to measure their productivity by adding up the lines of code being developed. This even became a common acronym used by managers – LOC. As software engineering has matured as a discipline, however, and as software engineers have come to appreciate the importance of both front-end loaded requirements and design work, as well as the need to minimize the LOC in a typical software project, this productivity measurement approach has become less popular and less frequently used.

- *Correctness Concerns*: Software engineers have come to understand that simplicity and care in module design are absolutely essential if the module is to work correctly. The principle of correctness dictates that software modules must be designed in a way that absolutely ensures that the final product is correct.

Today, most software engineers follow common methodologies; but a major problem with large software, such as the software running on your PC at home, is that there are too many flaws! Users of PCs, for example, think nothing of dealing with crashes, and "blue screens," and other weird behavior. Fixing these flaws represents a major task for software engineers to improve in the coming years.

27: Operating Systems

Operating systems are like underwear – nobody really wants to look at them.

Bill Joy

The most common software we all use is the *operating system* on our computers and smart devices. The operating system begins to run when you power on your hardware. It provides the icons, desktop tray, sound, and screen background that we select for our personal computers, tablets, and mobile devices. It serves as the interface between you and your hardware so that you can type things into applications, print pictures, send text messages, and browse the Internet.

It is also the software that runs on larger computer *servers* that power resources such as websites. Professional systems administrators make their living selecting, configuring, and managing server operating systems. This would include performing all the necessary housekeeping and security tasks to keep their servers running properly. Some common operating systems you might be familiar with include:

- *Windows* – Windows is Microsoft's popular operating system for personal computers and many types of servers. Windows dominates the personal computer industry, in business settings, with global market shares estimated by some to be in the 90% range for personal computers. For many users, the Windows interface and associated set of services are synonymous with *computers*.

- *Linux* – Linux is a free, open derivative of the important UNIX family of operating systems invented at AT&T. UNIX was invented at AT&T and made freely available for use by other organizations. Linux is one of the most successful derivatives that began with a so-called Linux *kernel program* introduced by Linus Torvalds in 1991.

- *iOS* – This is Apple's popular mobile device operating systems that powers its iPhone and iPad products. The iconic iPhone and its associated use of apps downloaded to iOS from the iTunes website, changed the entire mobile industry when it was introduced. Perhaps the most innovative element of iOS is its allowance for *direct touch manipulation* using manual gestures by human beings. These gestures allow for human actions such as swiping, pinching, sliding, touching, and wiping – all of which have a specific, defined meaning in the operating system.

- *Android* – Google's popular mobile device operating system, also a derivative of the Unix family of operating systems. It was developed as an open alternative to Apple's more proprietary operating system approach.

Here is a schematic view of the major components in a typical operating system for a typical computer:

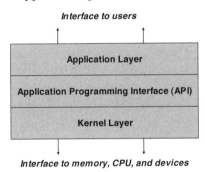

The three components shown above are the *application layer* that includes all of the applications that users can install, purchase, or use; the *application programming interface* (API) that applications use to connect to the underlying computer hardware; and the *kernel layer* which is the software that directly controls the hardware. The most important functions that these three operating system layers perform include the following:

- *Booting*: The booting function involves all the start-up functions required for a computer to be started.
- *Memory Management*: This includes all functions necessary to manage storage.
- *Program Execution*: This function controls the running of programs on the CPU.
- *Disk Access and File Systems*: This function organizes memory in a useful way.
- *Device Drivers*: These drivers provide interfaces to all external hardware.
- *User Interface*: This interface offers a view of the computer to its users.

Each of these important operating system functions is discussed in more detail in the sections below.

Booting: When you turn on or restart your computer, the operating system executes a set of initialization instructions called *boot* software. It is located in a portion of memory that cannot be changed called *read-only memory* or ROM. It then goes through a series of start-up tasks including checking to make sure your hardware is working properly, and then setting up your screen desktop. The diagram below shows the operating system boot process:

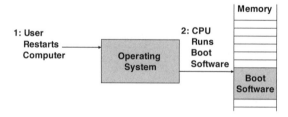

Memory Management: As program applications use areas of memory, data is written into the appropriate sections and then discarded; stacks are pushed and popped as needed, and memory is generally filled up with all sorts of data and programs that may or may not be important. Any area of memory that applications can change is referred to as *read-write memory*. One of the many different tasks that operating systems perform in order to keep applications functioning more smoothly is to clean up memory. One memory management task you may be familiar with involves *defragmentation* of memory. PC users often perform a defragmentation in order to make their programs execute better.

The diagram below shows the operating system locating and cleaning up fragments of memory:

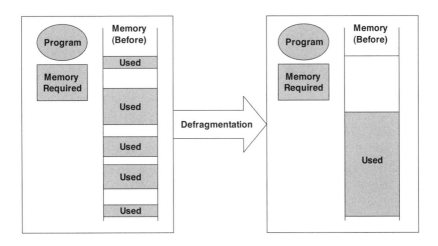

The program in the diagram requires a certain portion of memory to be available in a *contiguous block*. As you can see, the operating system does not have sufficient memory for this program, but after defragmentation, the block becomes available.

Program Execution: When programs are written and then loaded into memory for execution, it is the operating system that will provide the support necessary for this to occur. The operating system, in conjunction with any additional execution support software that might be made available as part of the programming language, will set aside sufficient memory, load up the computer, and the guide execution in a manner that will hopefully prevent the program from damaging other parts of the computer.

Disk Access and File Systems: Operating systems organize memory storage on the computer and on any off-line hardware such as *computer disks*. This organization is usually designed to create *file systems* that are logical to applications and even humans wishing to make use of such storage. The most typical structure used to organize file systems is the *hierarchical file structure*, where a so-called root node is created and used as the basis for many subsequent layers of file storage. A diagram of a typical hierarchical file system that organizes itself around so-called *directories*, which will be used to store files and other directories, is shown below:

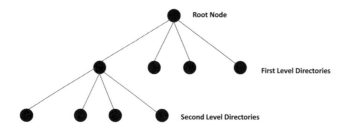

Device Drivers: The software on an operating system designed to provide an interface to external hardware such as a keyboard, mouse, or memory stick is called a *device driver*. Specific hardware will have specific device drivers, simply because the software must match up with the unique characteristics of that hardware. Anyone who has ever downloaded a driver for a printer, for example, knows the challenges in matching up specific device driver software with a specific operating system.

User Interface: Ultimately, users will differentiate operating systems by the characteristics of their *user interfaces*. This is especially obvious for human beings using operating systems, since the user interface is the totality of their experience with an operating system. When non-humans are using an operating system, such as in machine-to-machine applications, the user interface design will be evaluated in a less subjective manner.

28: Time Sharing and Multiprocessing

Machines take me by surprise with great frequency.

Alan Turing

Before the advent of personal computers in the 1980's, computing was performed on large systems called *mainframes*. These machines were expensive, and were often housed by companies and universities in large *computer centers*. Users would come to special rooms where devices called *terminals* were set up to allow them access to the mainframe computer. Below is a depiction of two users with terminals connected to a mainframe:

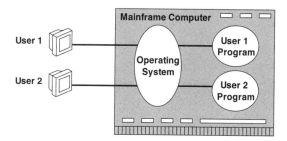

Each user is connected to the computer in order to run a program, but our current model of a computer involves only a single CPU to execute instructions. In such a scenario, the operating system has the job of creating a *multitasking* environment, where each of the users can share the same CPU to run programs *without having to wait*. The notion of wait time for users could be expressed in human terms, where milliseconds of delay would never be noticed.

The original solution to this problem involved the CPU providing alternating slices of time to each user. First one user would get a little time

131

slice of the CPU; then the other user would get a time slice; then the CPU would switch back to the first user (or to a third user); and this would continue on and on. By doing the switching really, really quickly, end users wouldn't notice that the CPU was being shared. The diagram below illustrates this concept of *timesharing* between two users:

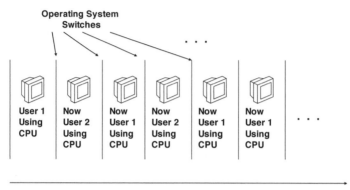

Keep in mind that the CPU executes instructions very quickly. Most processors can execute many, many millions of instructions per second. Computer manufacturers sometimes refer to the speed of a computer in MIPS (million instructions per second). Some current processors can run at tens of thousands of MIPS (do the math).

The reason we mention processor speed is that it allowed timesharing on mainframes to take advantage of the much slower reaction time for human beings. When two people, for example, were seated in front of a mainframe computer, they could enter data, read output, and run programs at a human speed that was much slower than the computer. Hence, by time sharing back and forth, the computer could create the illusion that it was dedicated to one user.

Modern computers still utilize time sharing to a degree. Most computers run multiple programs called *processes* at one time, but they are often not linked to different users. For example, if you are using a PC running a Microsoft Windows operating system, then by hitting the *control-alt-delete* (CTRL-ALT-DEL) command, you will get a listing of all the processes that are sharing the CPU at the current time. On a PC or laptop, there is obviously only one user, but the operating system is allowing these multiple processes to share the same CPU.

In modern computers, when multiple processes are running together and using software to share common resources, we refer to this as *multiprogramming*. As you might expect, however, modern computers often include multiple CPUs. In fact, complex military weapons systems often have a CPU that controls one aspect of the weapon, another CPU that controls another aspect of the weapon, and so on. Such computers are called *multiprocessor* computers, and they can execute more instructions more quickly.

In both multiprogramming and multiprocessing approaches, computer scientists can design systems that include processes that correspond to specific *tasks* that must be performed. This allows for much more complex systems to be designed in a modular manner. Suppose, for example, that a computer system on an airplane has one process that controls flight and another process that controls cabin temperature. Each process would run autonomously as follows:

Time	Flight Process	Temperature Process
	Execute Instruction Execute Instruction Execute Instruction . . .	Execute Instruction Execute Instruction Execute Instruction . . .

When you design systems with multiple processes, this introduces the possibility that different processes can communicate. Such exchange of information between processes is referred to as *inter-process communication*, and the sharing is usually referred to as sending and receiving *messages*.

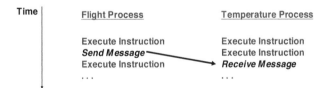

The ability to design processes that communicate introduces some interesting possibilities. Suppose, for example, that the temperature process checks the cabin temperature and if it gets too hot, then this could be a flight problem, so it would need to inform the flight process of the problem. This would involve inter-process communication between the temperature and flight processes and the exchange is shown below:

```
Time |        Flight Process              Temperature Process

              Execute Instruction         Check the temperature
              Execute Instruction         If temperature too hot then
              Execute Instruction    ┌──── Send Message to Flight Process
              Receive Message ◄──────┘     . . .
     ↓        . . .
```

A question that needs to be addressed by the system designer in the above scenario is how the flight process knows that a message has arrived from the temperature process. This could be done using an interrupt; but in many inter-process communication designs, the concept of a process *waiting* for a message introduces some interesting possibilities. For example, in the scenario shown above, one could imagine the flight process waiting for a message from the temperature process.

```
Time |        Flight Process              Temperature Process

              Execute Instruction         Check the temperature
              Execute Instruction         If temperature too hot then
              Start waiting for message   Send Message to Flight Process
               (Still waiting)            . . .
     ↓         (Still waiting)
              Receive Message ◄───────────┘
              . . .
```

You might wonder if it's really a good idea for a flight process on an airplane to just sit around waiting for a message from the temperature process! Perhaps, you might think, it would be better to design the processes in a different way. If you are thinking about this sort of thing, then you are starting to understand what it is like to design multiprocessing systems that intercommunicate.

More generally, however, multiprocessing on a single CPU has been replaced in modern computing with the more powerful notion of *distributed processing* on multiple, local CPUs. Furthermore, these distributed processes can execute remotely on entirely separate computers, perhaps communicating over a network such as the Internet. This is effectively what happens on most of the popular mobile apps that you have on your smart phone, and for virtually all on-line gaming systems.

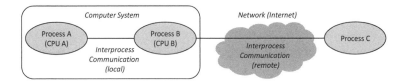

Generally, when computer scientists refer to different processes in execution and communicating toward some common objective, they do not draw the distinction between their underlying implementation. We will revisit many of the concepts of distributed processes communicating across multiple CPUs or over a network later in the book when we examine the Internet and mobile apps.

29: Semaphores and Synchronization

Prolific programmers contribute to certain disaster.

Niklaus Wirth

When two distributed processes want to utilize a common resource at the same time, interprocess communication provides an excellent means for working out some scheme that will avoid conflict. Suppose, for example, that two processes want to access a program that should only be used by one of them at a time. An example might be a document updating program, where you wouldn't want two processes updating at the same time. One solution to this problem involves a data structure known as a *semaphore*.

A familiar non-computing example that can help you understand the need for semaphores involves shared train tracks that must be somehow managed to avoid contention between different trains. Suppose, for example, that trains travel in the same direction along two parallel tracks that merge over a bridge that can only hold one train at a time.

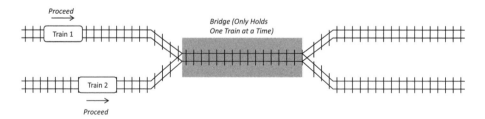

In order to make certain that both trains do not traverse the bridge at the same time, the first train to reach the bridge must set some sort of marker that the bridge is now in use. This marker, which is essentially a special type of semaphore, would then be viewed by the other train as a

136

warning to not try to cross the bridge. More specifically, it would be used as a safety mechanism to avoid contention for the shared resource, namely the bridge, that can only be used by one train at a time. If both trains try to set the marker at the same time, then there must be some sort of decision function that only allows one or the other to proceed, but never both.

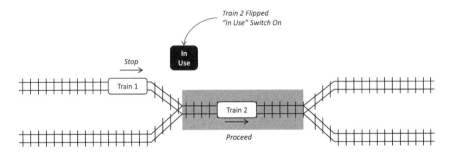

Once the first train is then finished with the shared resource (that is, it has crossed the bridge successfully), it can then reset the marker so that the other train can use the shared resource. Presumably, the other train has been delayed while the shared resource is in use, so it will then be able to proceed once the marker has been reset. Obviously, the second train would then set the marker to "In Use" once it begins to cross the bridge.

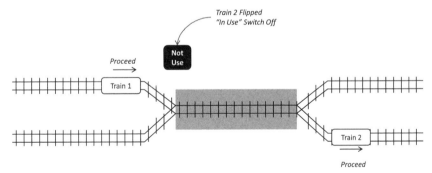

In computer science, the simplest type of semaphore is known as a *binary semaphore*. It works through a pair of operations commonly referred to by computer scientists as P (also referred to as *signal*) and V (also referred to as *wait*). The P operation *acquires* a resource by setting a semaphore variable to 0 (just as the train in our example above set the marker to "In Use"). The V operation *releases* that same resource by resetting the semaphore variable back to 1 (just as the train reset the marker to "Not Use"). Below is a depiction of the V release operation with a binary semaphore that has been set to 0.

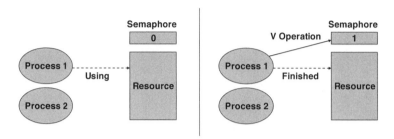

You can see that while the first process is using the resource, the semaphore value is set to 0. This makes it clear that the resource is in use. When that process is finished with the resource, then it performs a V (release) operation on the semaphore, thus setting it back to 1. Below is a depiction of the second process performing a P (acquire) operation with the binary semaphore:

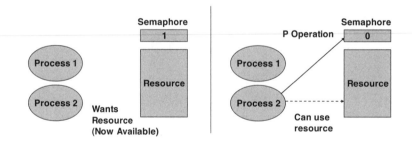

Semaphores are useful to programmers trying to solve problems involving what is known as *synchronization*. Whenever shared resources are available to multiple processes, all sorts of possible synchronization problems could emerge. To deal with more complex situations, a so-called *counting semaphore* might be used. What this involves is a semaphore that can have value 0, or some number greater than zero – based on the count.

To illustrate the use of a counting semaphore in solving synchronization problems, imagine that you have two distributed processes known as a *producer* and a *consumer*. This is a classic model in computer science because the notion of one process producing some resource or information, and another process consuming or using that output, matches so many different situations, especially in operating system design.

   If we suppose that items produced are placed into a container from which the consumer will obtain the items, and that these operations cannot be done to the container at the same time, then we might use a counting semaphore to synchronize this operation. The way this would work would be for an empty container to correspond to a counting semaphore set to zero. The consumer would know to wait on any zero value for this semaphore. On the other hand, if the semaphore is set to the maximum size of the container, then the producer would know to wait until some items are consumed. Upon each consumer item, the semaphore would be decremented, and on each produced item, the semaphore would be incremented.

   One classic type of synchronization problem that arises in distributed processing is known as *deadlock*. A deadlock condition emerges amongst a group of processes when they are all waiting for some action that will not occur as long as they all wait. Two cars at an intersection, both waiting for the other to proceed, are an example of a deadlock condition if they both continue to wait. A second type of synchronization problem is known as *livelock*, which occurs when processes are performing some action, but will never make any progress if they all continue to do the same thing.

   Computer scientists often use a problem known as the *dining philosophers* to illustrate deadlock and livelock. The way the problem works is that a group of philosophers are seated around a table; exactly one fork is placed between each of them, and a bowl of spaghetti sits in front of each person. The idea is that each philosopher is either thinking, or eating, in which case, two forks are needed. But obviously, there are not enough forks for everyone to be eating at once. Here is the depiction:

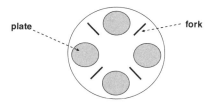

Suppose that you instruct each of the philosophers to begin by picking up the fork to their immediate left, and to then wait until the fork to the right becomes available. It should be obvious that this would lead immediately to a deadlock condition, where none of the philosophers would be able to ever eat. (We assume that they cannot communicate or see each other!)

If we modify the approach and tell each philosopher to pick up the fork to their immediate left, and to then wait exactly two minutes to see if another fork becomes available. If not, then the left fork should be placed back down on the table for one minute, after which the process should start again.

Think about this: If every philosopher starts at the same time, then do you see how they would never make progress? The result would be an infinite loop of actions where no philosopher makes any progress toward their combined goal. This condition effectively illustrates the concept of livelock.

30: Windows and UNIX

Unix is simple. It just takes a genius to understand its simplicity.

Dennis Ritchie

Starting in the 1990's, computer users began to prefer a family of operating systems referred to collectively as *Windows*. Built by *Microsoft*, the Windows design evolved with the needs of users and their PCs. Thus, as the use of the PC in the home and business grew dramatically through the 1990's, so did the success and fortunes of both Windows and Microsoft. Also, as midrange computers called *servers* became more popular, Windows evolved to address that market as well. (Servers are smaller than mainframes, but larger than PCs, and provide different types of services to multiple users.)

The first influential operating system design from Microsoft involved an operating system called *MS-DOS* created for the IBM PC in the 1980's. The acronym DOS stood for "disk operating system." To make MS-DOS more usable, Microsoft created a *graphical user interface* (GUI), which became the hallmark of Windows operating systems.[3] Thus, in this early incarnation, the MS-DOS operating system would control the hardware, and the Windows GUI would provide a visual view of the machine to users. Such a *layered view* of functionality is the most familiar and common representation of operating system architecture one finds in computer science.

---

[3] Most computer scientists agree that the graphical user interface was first introduced on a mass scale to customers by Apple with their early Macintosh system. This work, in turn, derived many of its ideas from research performed by the Xerox Corporation in the early 1980's, which included the invention of the mouse.

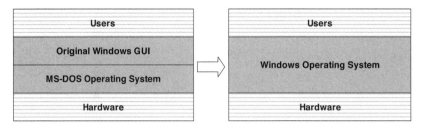

"Early Configuration"   *"Modern Configuration"*

As PC and server usage evolved, the need to include MS-DOS in the operating system architecture disappeared, and Windows became a fully functioning operating system on its own for PCs and servers. Windows now includes the familiar icon-clad GUI as well as support for the required underlying hardware and system controls. Versions of Windows that you may be familiar with include Windows Vista, Windows XP, Windows 2000, and Windows Mobile (for smart phones). Some characteristics of the Windows family of operating systems are listed below.

Proprietary Software: Windows is an example of a system that is designed by programmers who agree, as part of their employment at Microsoft, to keep the details of the software secret. In other words, users of Windows are not allowed to see how Windows software was specifically written. This common approach allows Microsoft and any other software companies following a similar strategy to protect their investment and to prevent companies from copying their software.

Security Bugs: Windows has had a poor reputation through the past decade of having many bugs in its code. Some of these bugs allow *hackers* to gain access to Windows computers without the proper credentials. Some programmers would attribute these bugs to the fact that the code base is proprietary. Their argument is that by not allowing people to inspect the software in the operating system, it simply does not receive enough review. Perhaps a more reasoned view is that software engineering has not reached the maturity level sufficient to produce any large software system without bugs.

Software Patches: To deal with these bugs in its code, Microsoft has had to create processes for adding fixes to the software known as *patches*. A patch is a piece of software that modifies, removes, or skips around a problem that cannot be easily fixed any other way, including direct removal of the bug. The diagram below illustrates how a patch might be used:

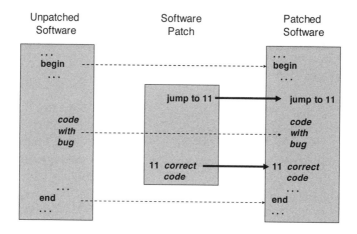

The way the patch works is that two specific insertions are provided for the code. First, a line of code is added in which the program logic is adjusted to jump to some location, designated in the example as memory location 11. The correct code is then inserted into that memory location, perhaps followed by some logic to return program control to the previous normal location.

Before Windows was invented, in the 1960's and 1970's, while computers were getting more powerful, the software running on them was pretty clumsy. Operating systems, in particular, were complex and tough to use. During this period, and long before Windows was created, a team of AT&T researchers led by Ken Thompson and Dennis Ritchie designed and began to use a small, elegant operating system which they dubbed the UNIX operating system.

UNIX was unique at the time, because it was *not* developed by a company as a product to make money, but was instead developed by programmers trying to make their work easier. The result was an elegant piece of software that remains important today. Apple's iPhone, for example, runs a version of UNIX nearly forty years after the operating system was invented!

The basic structure of UNIX can be viewed in terms of a layered model as having three parts: the *application level*, the *system call interface*, and the *kernel*. Thus, for example, processes running at the application level utilize UNIX features by making system calls through the system call interface to kernel-level utilities as shown below:

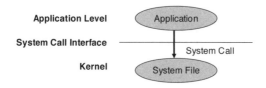

The original interface provided to programmers for UNIX was through a special program called a *shell*. The UNIX shell offered direct user access to the underlying computer in a particularly elegant manner. Specifically, the UNIX shell was designed in a structured manner based on computer science research at the time that was focused on languages. As a result, users of UNIX could actually write shell programs to accomplish their work. Below is an example of how a typical UNIX shell program looked (and still looks):

```
#!/bin/sh        -- first line in shell programs
clear            -- clears terminal screen
echo $path       -- prints value path variable
ls - al          -- lists current directory
```

Shell programs might look tedious to current computer users, but they provide a level of control that can be quite powerful to knowledgeable programmers. Suppose, for example, that you were trying to search the computer for some particular file. At the time, this would be a laborious, manual process. (Remember, UNIX was introduced long before you had Windows systems with a search button!) So users could write small shell programs called scripts that would do the work for them.

This was viewed at the time as a major advance, and it has since led to many of the basic operating system tools we all know and use today. If users wanted to then delete files that had some basic property, then the program could be extended to perform this action. In contrast, on a current operating system, if the point-and-click functions available to users do not provide the type of function desired, then the only option involves a long manual process. Some additional key features of UNIX are discussed below.

C Programming Language: From the beginning, UNIX has been tightly linked to a programming language developed at AT&T by Brian Kernighan and Dennis Ritchie called C. Before UNIX, it was rare to imagine an operating system that could be written in a programming language that would compile and run on *that* operating system! (Think about that one for a minute.) But the UNIX researchers were successful in developing ways for the operating system to be built using small modules called *software tools* that could then be used to develop additional modules. The result was something very close to what computer scientists now refer to as *machine learning*. In an earlier chapter, you saw an example of a C++ program (a derivative language of C), but below is a classic C program example to give you an idea of what the code looks like:

```c
#include <stdio.h>
int main ()
{
  printf( "Simple example C program.\n")
  getchar();
  return 0;
}
```

Open Source Software: UNIX is also an example of an *open source* system whose code is not, for the most part, considered a secret. Hence, computer scientists are well aware of the details in the system call interface and underlying kernel. Applications are often written by companies that prefer to keep their code secret, but the norm in UNIX is to make things open. This is a popular view with most programmers, but it does come with some baggage. For example, in open source systems such as UNIX, the presence of security bugs becomes known to all very quickly. While this leads eventually to fixes, it can be a painful process for anyone who depends on the open source code on a day-to-day basis.

Version and Variants: UNIX began as a single piece of software at AT&T, but it quickly branched into many, many different *versions*. Furthermore, as different groups took UNIX and tailored the code to their own special needs, the result was a series of new UNIX systems that computer scientists refer to as *variants*. So, just as biologists trace the origins of species to common roots that then branch off in different directions, so have computer scientists traced the development of UNIX to many newer derivative systems. Your mobile smart phone is most likely running one of these UNIX derivative versions.

31: Databases

Errors using inadequate data are much less than those using no data at all.

Charles Babbage

The concept of storing information in a structured manner has been part of computing since its origin. From the earliest days of computing, users created and used so-called *data banks*, whose storage was limited by the amount of memory that was available – usually not too much. A Macintosh computer in 1984, for example, might have cost you a few hundred dollars extra for an upgrade to *512K* of memory. Today, that amount is not much bigger than the size of a PowerPoint presentation.

As computing evolved, the need to store data for use by applications, systems, networks, end-users, and the like increased dramatically. In fact, a current trend in computing involves the storage and manipulation of huge amounts of data in gigantic stores referred to by the generic tag: *big data*. To understand how such data storage and processing works, we have to examine the underpinning of *database technology* which provides the building blocks for the storage, manipulation, and usage of structured data.

Let's begin our discussion by supposing that we want to create some convenient way to describe the students in your class, including their similarities and differences. Without a computer, you might just scribble all of this information down on a piece of paper. If we represented this data in an unstructured manner on a computer, then we would use a program such as a word processor or notepad-type program to enter it all in some unspecified way, without showing the *relationships* between the different stored data elements.

One way of viewing data with literally no relationship between the data elements is to depict it in a scattered manner as shown below:

Stephanie 914803

13 100292 Female

14 Alicia

Male

Lee Female 13

234877 Matt

14

Female 566512

Data represented in this unstructured manner may not always be easy to use. For example, to determine which locker numbers correspond to which students in the above case, you would need some external information or context to make this connection. If, on the other hand, we wanted to make the data more usable by providing more structure, then we might do this by writing down the information about each student on a piece of paper using a table with rows and columns as follows:

Name	Age	Gender	Locker Number
Lee	13	Female	234887
Alicia	14	Female	100292
Matt	13	Male	566512
Stephanie	14	Female	914803

If we wanted to perform an analysis on this data, then we would have much better context in which to do this. Based on the structure of the presented data, you could determine the average ages of the female students, you could determine who had the highest and lowest locker numbers, and so on. Since the data is written on paper, however, we would still have to perform our analysis manually with our eyeballs, or with pencil and paper. If we wanted to use a computer to provide assistance in our analysis, then we would enter the data into a program called a *database*.

The most common type of database is known as a *relational database*, so-named because the information is structured based on the "relationship" between the stored elements. Relational databases have become among the most common and important computing structures in the world, as nearly everything we all do every day is either stored or compared with some database that is stored and used on the Internet.

If the example table above were implemented as a database, the rows would be referred to as *database records*. Relational databases generally require that each record be unique so that something in each column is unique. As you can see, the example above does have all unique records. Relational databases also generally ignore the order of the columns, so that the above information would really not change if it looked like this:

Name	Gender	Age	Locker Number
Lee	Female	13	234887
Alicia	Female	14	100292
Matt	Male	13	566512
Stephanie	Female	14	914803

Database Rows

Database Columns

When a database is being accessed on a computer, this is done via a procedure known as a *database query*. Queries are often categorized by the type of operation involved. One categorization might partition queries into ones that change or "write" information into the database, and ones that view or "read" information into the database. More specifically, the most typical sorts of operations performed on a database include the following:

- *ADD*: Adding information to a database (categorized as a write operation since it changes the database).
- *RETRIEVE*: Obtaining information from a database (categorized as a read operation since it does not change the database).
- *UPDATE*: Making changes to information in a database (obviously categorized as a write operation).
- *DELETE*: Removing information from a database (also obviously categorized as a write operation).

This partitioning of database operations into read and write types is important, because some databases might be considered perfectly fine for users to view, but not to change, or vice versa. Thus, for example, *access controls* might be put in place to allow everyone to read the database, but that only authorized users can make changes.

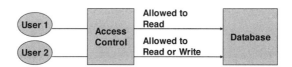

   This access control approach is viewed as a *security control* on the database. Businesses spend a great deal of time making certain that sufficient security exists to protect sensitive information from unauthorized viewers. When sensitive information is compromised from a database, the implication can be bad – especially if that sensitive information includes financial data.

   A consideration in the implementation of databases involves assurance that all operations performed on the database are *atomic*. This means that if you start an operation on a database, it either finishes completely or has no effect at all. Computer scientists describe this requirement by introducing a concept known as *database validity*. Here's an example to help explain:

   Suppose that your Mom or Dad has a checkbook that is balanced. This implies that all deposits, fees, and written checks have been entered into the checkbook, and that the subtotal balance is written in. A checkbook in this state is said to be *valid*. If we make sure that all changes to the checkbook are atomic, this will make sure that we don't do some partial operation like entering in a check, but forgetting to subtract the balance. Doing so would leave the database into an *invalid* state.

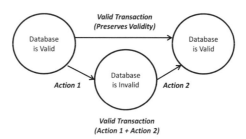

   The state diagram above illustrates this validity concept in database transactions. It is possible for a single transaction to preserve the validity of the database. For example, a user reading records on a database without making any changes is a perfectly valid transaction that will not leave the database in a state that is either incorrect or corrupt.

However, there are actions that can be performed on a database that will leave it in an invalid, intermediate state. If another action or sequence of actions is performed that will return the database to validity, then we refer to that full sequence of actions as a valid transaction.

Popular examples of modern *database management systems* include the following:

- *MySQL*: Pronounced "*My Sequel,*" this is the most popular, open source relational database system in use today.
- *SQLite*: This is a small, open source database management system that is popular as an embedded component in client software such as browsers.
- *Oracle*: This is the generic name for both the database management system as well as the corporation responsible for its design, development, and support.
- *IBM DB2*: This is IBM's popular family of database products for UNIX and Windows systems.

As more and more information is made available on the Internet, new database techniques will continue to be developed for storage and organization of data. At the root of these techniques, however, the basic notion of structured data being stored in a manner that allows one to perform analysis using relations between entities is likely to remain for a long time.

32: Cryptography

We in science are spoiled by the success of mathematics. Mathematics is the study of problems so simple that they have good solutions

Whitfield Diffie

An important consideration in computer science involves the *security* of computer systems. Security involves the protection of systems from malicious activity known as *hacking*. When a system is hacked, some individual or group exploits a weakness in the target system to bring about the desired result. A common exploit involves hackers gaining unauthorized access to information that they should never see, such as credit card numbers.

Most computer security experts agree that there are basically three primary threats to computer systems from hackers:

- *Denial of Service* – this involves a malicious individual or group overwhelming some website, server, or network with more volume that it can handle. The result is that it becomes unavailable for normal use. A technique known as a *distributed denial of service* (DDOS) attack has been all too common, especially when it is performed from a collection of hacked computers called a *botnet*.

- *Degradation* – this involves a malicious change or insertion into some target, thus reducing the integrity of that target. The most common method for integrity attacks involves *malware* insertions into target systems. Popular techniques for inserting malware include tricking someone into clicking on a website that includes malware, a process known as *phishing*.

- *Disclosure* – this involves important or secret information being stolen from an individual or group. When this occurs for an

151

individual, we say that that person's *privacy* has been compromised. When the private details of someone's life become compromised, we often say that their *identity* has been compromised.

Cryptography is used primarily to address this third threat involving disclosure and privacy compromise. It is the most common security technique used by computer scientists, even though it is not effective in addressing other types of attacks such as denial of service. It is best used to prevent hackers from obtaining unauthorized access to information, doing so by jumbling information in a clever way so that casual readers cannot understand what is written.

Computer scientists refer to the process of jumbling information as *encryption*, and to process of de-jumbling that same information as *decryption*. Both the encryption and decryption processes are enabled for use by a special piece of information known as a *key*. The basic schema for how encryption and decryption work together is sketched below:

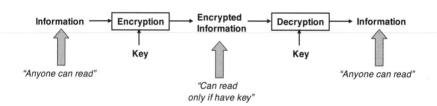

The use of cryptography generally assumes that someone owns a piece of sensitive information and protects that information by encrypting it with a key. That key information is then kept secret, and is only shared with those who have a right to view the information. So if someone named Alice wants to make sure that only she and her friend Bob can read that information, then she will encrypt it with a key, and will then only share the key with Bob. This process of handling keys is known to computer scientists as *key management*.

Let's now recall our use of binary numbers to illustrate an actual cryptographic algorithm with keys. What we'll do is use the binary XOR function for encrypting and decrypting binary information. Remember that the XOR function has the following truth table for two inputs:

XOR Truth Table

Input	Input	Output
0	0	0
0	1	1
1	0	1
1	1	0

If we make the first input in the XOR function the information to be encrypted and the second input the key, then the output will be decrypted. Let's assume that we're encrypting eight bit words and that we select a key at random. So here is an example encryption and decryption process using an input word, a random key (say, 0110 1110), and then the corresponding encrypted information:

Original Information	0011 1010	**Bitwise XOR of Original**
Key	0110 1110	**Information and Key**
Encrypted Information	0101 0100	
Key	0110 1110	**Bitwise XOR of Encrypted** **Information and Key**
Original Information	0011 1010	

The way to understand the XOR cryptographic function is to look at each bit, one at a time. Start with the rightmost '0' bit in the original information. That gets XOR'd with the rightmost '0' bit in the key to produce the rightmost '0' bit in the encrypted information (because 0 XOR 0 = 0). If we continue along from left to right, we can see how the information is encrypted. Once we've completed the encryption, notice that using the same key and the same XOR function, we can decrypt each bit from right to left producing the original information.

Note that the cryptography shown above assumes that use of a common or *single-key* for the creator and receiver of encrypted information. One problem that arises in single-key cryptography is that two entities might not have an opportunity to exchange key information in advance. For instance, if you wish to purchase something on-line, you certainly do not want to go through the advance process of registering key information with the web site. It would be easier to buy the item in a regular store!

Luckily, a more flexible type of cryptography known as public-key cryptography was invented many years ago, and it provides exactly the type of arrangement that is useful for on-line security. The way public-key cryptography works is that all participants who wish to encrypt or decrypt information with others must have a special type of algorithm that will generate the following two related cryptographic keys:

- *PA*: This is the public key for Alice that will be made available to every other participant. You can think of this process of making this available as being similar to Alice making her phone number or email address available to others.

- *SA*: This is the secret key for Alice that will be kept secret and not shared with anyone. In this sense, it is sort of like a secret password that must be protected carefully in order for the cryptography to work properly.

The way public and secret keys work is that if Alice encrypts some original, readable information known as *plaintext* with her public key, then the resulting unreadable information, known as *ciphertext*, can only be decrypted with the corresponding secret key. We can depict this process in cryptographic notation as follows (where the squiggly braces denote encryption and decryption):

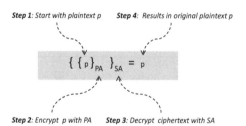

This concept is powerful, because it creates some useful protocol scenarios between entities. For example, if Alice is an Internet user and knows the public key of some website Bob, then she can encrypt her credit card information over the Internet to Bob as shown in the diagram below:

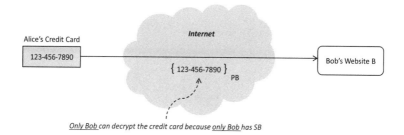

Only Bob can decrypt the credit card because only Bob has SB

Notice that as the encrypted credit card information is sent to Bob over the Internet, the only entity who can possibly decrypt the ciphertext to read the credit card is Bob. This situation gives Alice the confidence she needs to actually send private information over the Internet in a way that will not compromise her credit card information or her identity.

Computer scientists have used these basic cryptographic concepts to help people buy items securely on the Internet, and to send and receive information privately on the Internet. In fact, without cryptography, the case could be made that there would be no electronic commerce or even use of credit cards on the Internet.

33: Networks

A distributed system is one in which the failure of a computer you didn't even know existed can render your own computer unusable.

Leslie Lamport

Computers exchange information over *networks*. At the simplest level, a network consists of some *communication medium*, such as a wire, that accepts output from one computer and passes it along as input to another.

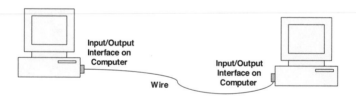

In the simplest network set-up, one computer writes information to a memory location that is mapped to its input/output interface. The binary information then travels over the wire and is connected to the input/output interface of the receiving computer. Computer scientists refer to this type of network set-up as *point-to-point*. Your home personal computer might be connected to a printer in this manner.

If we grow the size of our simple point-to-point network to include three different computers, perhaps each with two input/output interfaces, the resulting network might look like this:

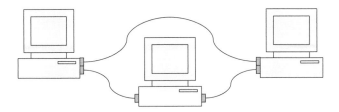

    Apart from having more wires and connections, this network is still pretty simple. Your family television, set-top box, and digital video recorder might be connected roughly in this manner. If we grow our network to four machines, the point-to-point connections become only slightly more complex, but still manageable.

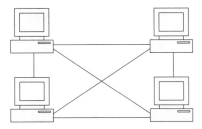

    Notice that in a network containing only two computers, we needed one connection between the two end-points or *network nodes*; for three computers, we needed a total of three connections between the nodes; and for four computers, we needed a total of six connections between the nodes. This suggests that the number of connections is growing faster than the number of computers. Computer scientists express concern when this happens, because such a growth condition could lead to problems when the number of computers really grows large, such as on the Internet. Below we show the number of connections required for six computers:

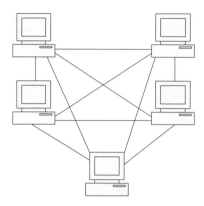

This network requires ten connections, and by now, you should see a pattern, potentially expressible by some mathematical expression. For 2 nodes, we needed (2 – 1) = 1 connections; for 3 nodes, we needed (3 – 1) + (2 – 1) = 3 connections; for 4 nodes, we needed (4 – 1) + (3 – 1) + (2 – 1) = 6 connections; and for 5 nodes, we needed (5 – 1) + (4 – 1) + (3 – 1) + (2 – 1) = 10 connections.

Example: Using the pattern above, show how many point-to-point connections would be needed for seven nodes.

Answer: We would need (7 – 1) + (6 – 1) + (5 – 1) + (4 – 1) + (3 – 1) + (2 – 1) connections which is 6 + 5 + 4 + 3 + 2 + 1 = 21 connections.

It turns out that n different nodes, there will be exactly: (n * (n – 1)) / 2 lines required. To demonstrate the use of this equation, we can see that if n = 2, then there are (2 * (2 – 1)) / 2 or 1 required line; if n = 7, then there are (7 * (7 – 1)) / 2 or 21 connections; and so on.

As you can imagine, large point-to-point networks can quickly become a rat's nest of connections. Computer scientists have therefore tried to create better ways to design networks that scale more effectively. They do this by creating special networking procedures called *protocols*. A network protocol is an agreed-to series of steps that computers follow to send and receive information.

The most basic of all computer network configurations supporting protocol communications is the *client-server configuration*. In such a configuration, one node of the network serves the others by providing necessary services for different nodes to accomplish whatever sort of task or sharing is desired.

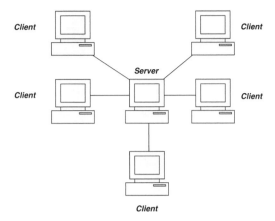

Note the advantage of the client-server model in terms of expandability. When a new node is to be added to the network, the server simply adds one new connection to that client and can then serve as the means by which different clients can communicate. Such a linear growth model is ideal for large networks such as the Internet.

For example, if one client wishes to exchange photos with another client, then they might both connect to a common photo exchange server. The server would then provide the necessary services for the two clients to exchange photos in an arrangement referred to as a *store-and-forward* approach.

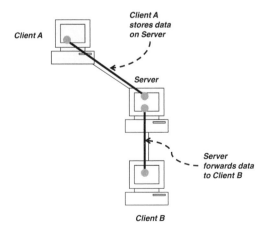

Email services also work in a store-and-forward manner where a sender creates and transmits an email which is stored by intermediate servers along the way. In many cases, when sufficient email is available for batch transmission, the entire batch is then forwarded along to the recipients. This is acceptable because no one expects email to be an immediate, real-time service like voice communications between two human beings.

Alternatively, if the server simply provides so-called pass-through services that allow clients to communicate directly, then the result is a so-called *peer-to-peer* arrangement. For example, two clients wishing to perform video chatting might each install the appropriate client and then connect over a server that provides the necessary pass-through for the clients to communicate. Depending on the specific methods employed, peer-to-peer arrangements might not require any type of intermediate servers.

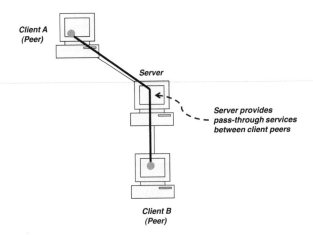

Certain types of file sharing services on the Internet such as *bit torrent* work in a peer-to-peer manner. When the single server in a client-server arrangement supporting store-and-forward, peer-to-peer, or some other arrangement, is replaced with a more complex set of computing and connection services, perhaps as part of an *Internet Service Provider* (ISP) network, then we generally view clients as being configured in a so-called *client-network* arrangement, much as you would see with home computers connected into a service provider's network.

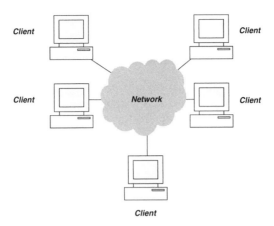

The different types of networks that exist in practice today include the following:

- *Local Area Network (LAN):* This is a network that generally spans a modest distance, usually within a home, building, or campus, such as at company, college or university. Some LANs have grown to span larger distances in companies that have grown, but generally a LAN is a small network. *Ethernet* is an important technology that is used in most local area networks.

- *Metropolitan Area Network (MAN):* This is a network that generally exists across some number of miles (less than thirty), often within a city or geographic area – hence the name. Many service providers are beginning to emphasis MAN provision in areas where there are a sufficient number of customers.

- *Wide Area Network (WAN):* This is a large network that spans a wide area, perhaps global, such as the Internet, that usually includes computing and networking infrastructure from Internet Service Providers. WAN management is usually quite complex and requires various types of network management tools.

In any LAN, MAN, or WAN, two of the most fundamental technical considerations involve the specific *protocol* used for exchange of information between nodes on a network, and the means for providing *addresses* to the various nodes on the network. Thus, if a client personal computer is connected over some network to a server that is also connected to the network, then the question arise about which steps should be used to exchange information, as well as how to locate the server and personal computer.

In recent years, protocol communications and the associated addressing have become standardized on everything from LANs to WANs to even your mobile services. The new standard protocol is known as the *Internet Protocol* (IP), and this will be examined in more detail in the next chapter.

34: Packets and the Internet

*Anyone who has lost track of time when using a computer
knows the propensity to dream, the urge to make dreams
come true and the tendency to miss lunch.*

Tim Berners-Lee

The standard *protocols* used by computers on a network to
communicate are based on a multi-stage delivery model that is
similar to the one used by the postal service for mail delivery.

Let's examine how mail is delivered. First, the sender puts a
letter in an envelope. The postal service then places this envelope into a
sack of envelopes. The sack is then placed inside a truck full of sacks.
Eventually, the sack is removed from the truck, the envelope is removed
from the sack, and the letter is removed from the envelope. This process is
shown below.

Letter	Envelope	Sack	Truck	Envelope	Letter
Placed In	Placed In	Placed In	Travels to	Pulled from	Pulled from
Envelope	Sack	Truck	Destination	Sack	Envelope

One way to describe this mail handling process is to view each step
as a *layer*. Thus, we would have a layer where letters are placed into and
pulled from envelopes; we would have another layer where envelopes are
placed into and pulled from sacks; and we would have a layer where sacks
are placed into and pulled from trucks.

Computer scientists would depict these different layers of
processing for network communications in a model drawing that would
look as follows:

In modern networks, information is arranged for delivery in a somewhat similar manner. Instead of sending letters inside envelopes, modern networks send information inside so-called *packets*. To make things efficient, the information being sent is generally broken up into smaller pieces, and placed inside many different packets. A file, for example, being sent from one computer to another over a network would be broken up into a series of packets which are re-assembled by the recipient upon delivery.

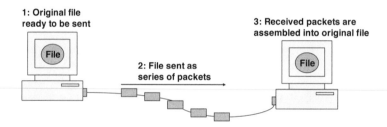

Just as with the postal service approach, packets are created with information about their point of origin, which is called the *source*, as well as information about their target location, which is called the *destination*. In particular, each packet is stamped with the *address* of the source and destination involved in any network transmission.

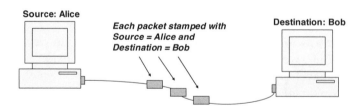

On the Internet, the agreed upon method for stamping packets with addresses is part of a protocol known as the *Internet Protocol* or just *IP*. Thus, the Internet can be viewed as a collection of end-points with IP addresses that send out streams of packets that find their destination via these addresses. When an IP connection is initiated by some end-point, we refer to that end-point's IP address as the *source address*. The IP address of the recipient of those packets is referred to as the *destination address*.

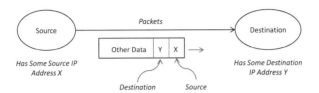

Source and destination addressing in IP are done to ensure that packets sent from a source find their way to the destination, potentially over many d5ifferent possible network paths. Other protocols have been designed to run in conjunction with IP to help ensure that this works. The most common one is referred to as the *Transport Control Protocol* (TCP). What TCP does is include numbers on each packet – so-called sequence numbers – that can be used by the receiving destination to reassemble what was sent from the source.

In order to understand how packets are really transferred on a network from a source to a destination, we must learn about devices called *routers* that read the destination address and point the packet off in the right direction. The way routers decide where to point incoming packets for delivery is based on a predetermined set of rules. These rules might be predetermined to send anything destined for Bob off on one interface, and anything destined for Mary off on another interface. The rules are preloaded into the router and stored in a so-called *routing table*. Below is a simple example table:

> **Routing Table:**
> **If Destination = Bob, then send out on Interface A**
> **If Destination = Mary, then send out on Interface B**

Now let's create a simple network example with one router that is loaded with the table above, and we can analyze whether the network will work properly.

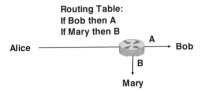

You can see that the router in the diagram accepts input from Alice, and based on the routing table entries, make the determination whether to route packets to Bob or Mary. Based on a cursory examination of this simple network, it looks like things will work out fine, as long as packets are stamped properly.

Amazingly, the entire Internet is based on the concept illustrated above. Every computer on the Internet has its own IP address, and when you try to connect to another computer (perhaps a Website), routers between you and that Web site will make decisions about how best to get packets to and from you and the Web site. The Internet Protocol is particularly powerful because it does not require any centralized authority to run it. Routers are set up, connected into networks, and they all help move information between sources and destinations.

To hide the complexity of all this routing and decision making on the Internet, computer scientists often represent the Internet pictorially as a *cloud*. Such visual depiction is intended to allow designers to explain aspects of the Internet without having to worry about its underlying details. Such use of abstraction allows for simpler explanations of complex ideas.

For example, if a computer scientist wanted to show that the endpoints on the Internet include PCs and servers, this would be done using an Internet cloud diagram with depicted endpoints as follows:

In reality, the Internet is itself a series of interconnected networks, many of which are operated by companies called *Internet Service Providers* or *ISPs*. These ISPs provide the on-ramps to the Internet that we are all used to in our daily lives. These come in the form of broadband connections into our home, large-scale Internet gateway connections for businesses, network connections to hosted Web servers for anyone providing Internet content, and mobile Internet connectivity for smart devices.

Drilling down a bit deeper into the design and operation of the Internet, you should know that the overall global network operates as a series of so-called *autonomous systems* (AS). These autonomous systems are numbered and are administered by their respective owners, which in many cases are the ISPs. Several protocols are then run across these autonomous systems to allow the Internet to function. One of these is known as the *border gateway protocol (BGP)*, which acts like the overall routing or traffic cop on the Internet.

Another important protocol that runs across the Internet is the so-called *domain name system* (DNS). This is the system that translates the familiar domain names you use every day such as *amazon.com* or *google.com* into their associated IP addresses, and then back again. This system requires a complex system of hierarchical relationships between different domain levels such as "dot-com" and "dot-net". These top-level domain levels are administered by designated authorities who must respond to queries by systems that wish to perform the desired translation.

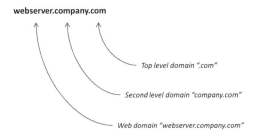

It is interesting to note that hackers, in recent years, have found the DNS protocol irresistible for their various pranks, because by mucking with DNS queries, the Internet can be made to operate in a strange, even non-functional, manner.

Above all other protocols, however, the *hypertext transfer protocol* (HTTP) is by far the most pervasive and influential of all. Invented in the mid-1990's by Tim Berners-Lee, it is the means by which web sites are coded and made available to viewers using programs known as *browsers*. To understand HTTP, you must recognize that the client-server model prevails in the communication, where your browser is the *HTTP client*, the web site (or web server) is the *HTTP server*, and the protocol is used to exchange *resources* such as files.

The most common resource involved in the HTTP protocol involves a so-called *hyper text markup language* (HTML) file that specifies how a given web page should be presented to the requesting user. The creator of a web site uses HTML to creatively define the layout, structure, orientation, content, color, audio and video elements, and other aspects of the web experience. When the browser connects to the web site, it obtains the HTML code over HTTP, and then uses that definition to render the web experience for the user.

We refer collectively to the billions of Web sites, browser clients, and coded HTML as the *World Wide Web* (www) or just the *Web*. It would be hard to identify an invention in computing that has had more impact on our lives recently than the invention of the Web. For most people, in fact, the Web *is* the Internet. There are, of course, many other important services such as *electronic mail* (email) that reside on the Internet and operate using the Internet protocol.

35: Mobile Apps

Every day sees humanity more victorious in the struggle with space and time.

Guglielmo Marconi

One of the more recent advances on the Internet involves *mobile* access to resources using smart devices such as the iPhone. While the infrastructure requirements to ensure full coverage across the globe are complex and require great investments by mobile service providers, the conceptual model for mobile Internet access over the air is simple. Mobile devices are designed to communicate over wireless radio frequencies to strategically-placed cell towers, which are connected to the Internet.

For many years, the primary purpose of cell site towers was to provide a means for people to use mobile phones to talk. Devices were created that would connect over the air to early second generation (2G), third generation (3G), and now fourth generation (4G) networks. Texting and email services soon became popular on mobile networks, and now we use mobile devices to access the Internet almost as frequently as we do with PCs. Such Internet access has made possible the creation and use of so-called *mobile apps* which are for everything from playing games to checking tomorrow's weather.

The designation app is a shortening of 'application', a term which has been used by computer scientists for many years. An application is a piece of compiled software that operates on a computer system, usually with a direct interface to some end-user, often a human being. Most of the time, applications do not provide underlying support services on a computer or network system, but rather provide some specific function – at least, when they are designed properly.

On mobile devices, applications are especially important because users have come to differentiate their mobile experience based on the types of specific functions that can be enabled on their device – and this is done by downloading *mobile apps*. The use of mobile apps has exploded to the point where customers of mobile devices often make their purchasing decisions based on the types of apps available for that device. The way mobile apps are distributed involves wireless download from an app store site to the requesting device. Mobile engineers often refer process to this as a download *over-the-air* (OTA).

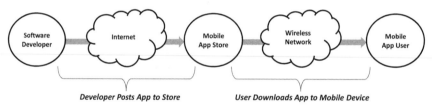

Developer Posts App to Store   *User Downloads App to Mobile Device*

The concept of developers creating and posting their apps to a store, basically, a mobile website, has revolutionized software distribution. In the past, software would be distributed on separate media such as compact discs and memory sticks, which limited the scope and scale of such distribution. It also required the use of physical media which was expensive to create and distribute.

In the early days of the Internet, for example, a company called America On-Line (AOL) flooded the entire United States with literally millions of CDs containing their registration software since this was the only method available to get the software mass distributed. Today, such distribution would obviously be done over-the-air on a mobile network directly to end-user mobile devices using an on-line app store.

As one would guess, apps must be targeted to specific operating system platforms. For example, if a developer is interested in writing applications for Apple products, then their software must be written for the applicable Apple operating system such as iOS. If, however, a developer is interested in writing applications for Android products, then their software must be written for that operating system.

The result has been a mobile app development, downloading, and usage ecosystem that is inconsistent across mobile platforms. This explains why your Android phone does not easily run iPhone applications. Instead, developers have to develop different versions.

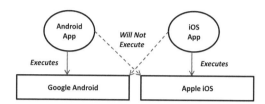

Most computer scientists view the mobile app revolution of the past few years as a glimpse into the future of how computing will affect our everyday and business lives. In particular, the idea that virtually anyone with some programming skill can create and distribute software that might be useful to a large audience is a stunning advance.

The two most popular app stores that are being used at the time of this writing are the following:

- *iTunes* – This is Apple's flagship app store, offering a large variety of apps and other types of content, especially music and video, to mobile subscribers. One important aspect of the iTunes approach is that Apple tries to provide some oversight as to the types of apps and content that are posted for download.

- *Google Play* – This is Google's Android marketplace app store, offering a growing variety of apps and content in an environment that is somewhat more permissive that Apple's approach. The result is a more interesting, but also possibly more dangerous (malware) environment for download.

In order to understand how mobile apps work on a network, we must first understand the idea of a so-called *client-server* interaction. In such an arrangement, two communicating processes, often on different systems, interact in a way that generally aligns the client as an interface for individual users to invoke services from the server. As such, you might think of the mobile app as a client that – when you click on it – reaches out over-the-air to a special server that is listening for such communication.

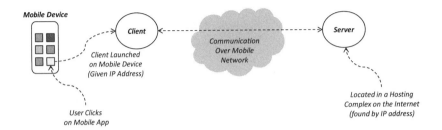

The way clients and servers find each other on mobile networks is by IP address. The initiating process has a so-called *source address* and the receiving process has a *destination address*. As such, the mobile app communication really is just an Internet communication, where the initial portion of the packet journey goes over-the-air from the mobile device to a local mobile service provider cell tower. These cell towers are then connected, essentially, to the Internet for delivery to the target destination.

One possible future for downloadable mobile apps involves their use on devices other than mobile phones, tables, and personal computers. For example, once every device and system in the home – television, furnace, locks, refrigerator, lighting, and the like – are all connected to mobile networks, then it will become possible for software developers to design and make available specific apps for the device.

As an example, imagine that you've purchased a refrigerator with a mobile connection, which allows you to monitor its temperature and view the contents via a camera. Developers might create apps that would perform functions such as checking whether you have certain items in the refrigerator, and if not – then the app would have these items delivered to your home.

Regardless of the specifics of how such general use of mobile apps will appear, it is obvious that the concept of dynamically downloading application software to a device over a mobile network is likely to be an important part of our lives for many years to come.

Index